Herman Linder with his 1934 North American All-Around Cowboy award. The bronze was donated by artist C.A. Beil of Banff, Alberta. It was the first of many bronze creations that Beil made for the Calgary Stampede. *Photo courtesy Glenbow Archives WA3252-3*

THE LINDER LEGEND
— The Story Of ProRodeo And Its Champion

THE LINDER LEGEND

—The Story Of ProRodeo And Its Champion

BY HARALD GUNDERSON

Published by Sagebrush Publishing, 327 Wainwright Road SE, Calgary, Alberta T2J 1H9. Tel: (403) 271-0875 or Fax: (403) 281-9570.

ISBN 0-9695792-2-5

First Printing: November, 1996

Canadian Cataloguing in Publication Data

Grateful acknowledgment is made to the following for permission to reprint previously published material:

- Cliff Faulknor, author, *Turn Him Loose!* Calgary, Alberta
- *Canadian Rodeo News*, Calgary, Alberta
- Canadian Professional Rodeo Association, Calgary, Alberta
- Professional Rodeo Cowboys Association, Colorado Springs, Colorado
- Calgary Exhibition and Stampede, Calgary, Alberta
- *ProRodeo Sports News*, Colorado Springs, Colorado
- Glenbow Archives, Calgary, Alberta
- Jack McCullough, Calgary, Alberta

Book design and electronic production by Signature West Communications and Publishing Inc., Calgary, Alberta

Proofreading by Cori Paul and Lee Gunderson

Printed and bound by Apache Superior Printing Ltd., Calgary, Alberta, Canada

NO TOC

Alan Young 1930–1989

Dedicated to the memory of Alan Young, rodeo cowboy and foreman of Pincher Creek Ranches, Pincher Creek, Alberta — and to rodeo cowboys and cowgirls and rodeo fans everywhere.

Herman Linder

DS Photo

An Attitude of Gratitude

There's one thing about horses that can't be said for humans — the really bad ones have a use, ending up with careers as bucking stock in rodeos.

That was the feeling of rodeo producer Herman Linder as he staged an early Edmonton, Alberta rodeo.

Speaking in 1951, Herman said a cowboy's life is pretty much a gamble. "Most are lucky if they make $2,000 or $3,000 a year — not counting expenses — although about fifteen cowboys in the world will make $20,000 a year in 1952."

Herman, a full-time rancher, horse buyer and rodeo producer said he got out of the bronco busting business with little more than a smashed knee and a chipped spine.

"I'm grateful to rodeo for a lot of things. Without that prize money, Agnes and I would never have been able to put together our ranch and cowherd. But that was in the 1930s where land was available for five dollars an acre and good range cows could be bought for fifteen dollars each," he said.

Introduction

Herman Linder. Cowboy!

By Ralph W. Murray, Canadian Professional Rodeo Association
General Manager, 1983-1995 (currently on medical disability leave)

One word can be used to describe Herman Linder. Cowboy!

From his broad Stetson hat to the tips of his riding boots, Herman is the cowboy's cowboy.

Rodeo achievements unequalled by his colleagues, loved by his fans, immortalized by the rodeo world, a leader in the farming and cattle ranching business, honoured by nations, communities and organizations throughout the world, all of which will be chronicled throughout the pages of this book.

Ralph Murray

Most importantly, from my perspective, Herman Linder helped lay the foundation and set the cornerstone for the sport of rodeo and where we are at today in the business.

As a young cowboy starting out, Herman quickly recognized that rodeo contestants should be better compensated for their talents and protected from those promoters who exploited cowboys for their own personal gain. He was part of a small band who met in Boston, Massachusetts in November, 1936 and staged a one-day strike for a better deal for the rodeo cowboy.

Thus, the Cowboys' Turtle Association was born, so-named because they were slow to get started and were ready to stick their necks out. The CTA evolved to the present day Professional Rodeo Cowboys Association which is closely affiliated with the Canadian Professional Rodeo Association, Australian Professional Rodeo Association and New Zealand Professional Rodeo Association. Many of their rules still bear the basics of the criteria initially set down by that fledgling group of cowboys in the late 1930s.

Herman's personal achievements as a rodeo cowboy will most likely never be matched and will stand as an eternal monument throughout the major historical societies that have inducted him into their respective Halls of Fame over the past eighteen years.

After hanging up his spurs and chaps in 1939, Herman continued to maintain a strong interest in the development and presentation of rodeo. Following the Second World War he began to produce rodeos on behalf of many agricultural societies throughout the Canadian West and was a prominent leader as an arena director and rodeo manager.

The Southern Alberta Rodeo Circuit flourished for twenty years as a result of his many innovations to the sport. A crowning achievement was the call to produce the Great Western Rodeo at Expo '67 in Montreal, Quebec. It was a great success.

It was a fitting tribute that my hometown of Medicine Hat, Alberta asked Herman to be guest of honour, parade marshall and officially open their fiftieth anniversary stampede in 1996. He had produced their stampede for many and many a year, starting in 1946.

He was a catalyst in developing that strong sense of pride and competition we observe today in our present-day stock contractors and rodeo producers, because this man set a high standard in the rodeo arena as a cowboy contestant and a rodeo showman.

Away from the rodeo infield he set a standard as a husband, a father, a rancher, a friend and exemplary citizen.

Herman is revered by all of us who have had the good fortune to walk in his shadow and share his company in the arena of life.

*Herman Linder ...
ready to start the Edmonton indoor rodeo.*

My Friend, Herman Linder

By Harald Gunderson

It has been sixty-five years since Herman Linder first wrote in a diary in 1932. And he has faithfully recorded entries each year since.

He was twenty-five years of age when he started to write about happenings at the ranch at Cardston, Alberta, his travels along the rodeo trail, the hard-fought struggles to improve the lot of the rodeo cowboy, and his personal initiatives to promote rodeo as a spectator sport.

Herman Linder and Harald Gunderson on the Linder range.

Examination of the Linder Diaries reveals a man whose love of family, community, ranching and rodeo knows no bounds. A tireless worker, a great optimist and one of limitless energy. He is a manifestation of the early days of the Canadian west; a vision under a cowboy hat.

It was the Linder touch that put him in six Cowboy Halls of Fame and it is the Linder touch that helps to spell success for rodeo today. He may not be there to ride a bronc or wrestle a steer, but the rodeo spirit he helped create is very much evident.

Herman would be the first to say that, in all the world of athletics, there is nothing quite like a rodeo. In no other sport are so many players likely to bite the dust with such thumping, bone-jarring spectacular spills.

His display case in the Cowboy Hall of Fame in Oklahoma City reveals trophies from three continents and four countries. For Herman, in the split-decade of 1929-'39, won rodeo prizes in the United States, Canada, Australia and England.

The pages of his diaries tell of his work on behalf of rodeo and identifies one of the top sports promoters in Canada. Here is an outstanding example of a top performer, later to become a top man in the business and production end of the sport in which he became famous. And he left rodeo with both gentleness and integrity intact.

Wrote the late Guy Weadick, founder of the Calgary Stampede: "Herman's history shows that real application, hard work and clean living count much for success, in the dangerous work of a cowboy contestant."

Said Justice Kenneth Moore in a 1981 address to the fiftieth annual Rangemen's Dinner in Calgary: "Herman Linder has been to rodeo what Babe Ruth was to baseball, what Gordie Howe was to hockey and Knute Rockne was to football — a legend. He is a builder of rodeo and hailed by many as Canada's King of the Cowboys."

Oldtimers say Herman had so much command of a horse, he made riding saddle broncs look easy. All he had to do was sit up straight and do it right. With his own grace and style, he was the picture perfect bronc or bareback rider; he was the cowboy on the bucking horse, the emblem of rodeo that many in Canada came to admire.

I have known Herman for twenty-five years. He is modest to a fault and, at eighty-nine years of age, a walking, talking museum of rodeo.

He is, indeed, a Legend in his time.

Herman Linder stands beside a showcase holding some of his memorabilia after his induction into the Cowboy Hall of Fame in Oklahoma City, Oklahoma, December, 1981. Included in the display are: a Sydney, Iowa championship saddle;, two international competition cups from Australia; a cigarette case (never used) from His Royal Highness The Prince of Wales; and two Calgary Stampede gold belt buckles.
Bob Everly Photo.

Table of Contents

Artist Robert Magee, right, with Herman and Adeline Linder during the 1995 unveiling of Winning It All, *the book's front cover painting.*   *Lee Gunderson Photo*

Winning It All At Calgary

The cover painting, *Winning It All*, shows Herman Linder aboard the big Ray Knight sorrel horse, Easy Money, which he spurred to fame at the Calgary Stampede in 1934. He was first in the Canadian saddle bronc, bareback, and steer riding events and North American and Canadian All-Around Champion cowboy at Calgary that year.

Winning It All is part of a collection of eighteen original oil paintings by acclaimed western artist, Robert Magee. The collection is aptly titled, *Legendary Horsemen — Images of the Canadian West.*

The paintings were commissioned by D.K. "Doc" Seaman, honourary chairman of the board of the Western Heritage Centre Society, Cochrane, Alberta. The prominent Calgary businessman and rancher graciously donated the collection to the Centre and it is displayed in a permanent gallery.

As a boy in Toronto, the romance of the old West captured Magee's imagination, as did the horses of a local international racing stable. Today, his deepening and developing interest in the people and horses of the West have coalesced in his art. The result is work of unusual quality and interest.

Magee's talent, and insistence on visual truth, brought critical success. His photograph collection, *The Classical World of Horses*, was published in New York. In 1990, he was invited by the Kentucky Horse park to hold a one-man exhibition of his paintings and photographs at the William Kenton Gallery of the International Museum of the Horse.

Then Magee trekked west to live in Calgary, at the foothills of the great plains. As he says: "The horse belongs in the West, here it is the star of the show." More recently, Magee's art has taken a predictable step in his paintings of Western history. "Only a small, part of the history of the horse and horsemen of the Canadian West has been recorded in pictures," he notes. "It is my ambition to continue their heritage in my future paintings."

D.K. "Doc" Seaman of Calgary, left, with Herman Linder.   *Lee Gunderson Photo*

Magee will travel far in the interest of authenticity. He visits museums. He walks the site of a subject to observe the terrain and make landscape studies. He consults with historians and expert horsemen. He studies the chronicles of contemporaries, gathers recollections passed down orally, searches out artifacts and clothing items, determines which breed of horse was where and when. First the understanding, then its expression.

Magee is working with the Royal Canadian Mounted Police Centennial Museum in Regina, Saskatchewan, on the commemoration of the one hundred and twenty-fifth anniversary of the North-West Mounted Police (1873-1998). A special exhibition of twenty-five paintings on *The North West Mounted Police Horses and the Great March West* will open at the MacKenzie Art Gallery in Regina in June, 1998.

The exhibition will then travel and be on view at major museums in the United States and Canada. Robert Magee's paintings of this historic event will be recorded in a publication scheduled for release in the fall of 1998.

Canada's Pete Knight on Dempsey - Sheridan, Wyoming - July, 1932.

Jack McCulloch Collection

Rodeo — A King Of The Sports World

"... Rodeo today is the way I hoped it would some day be. Early on, cowboys didn't have a good reputation. When we got organized, if somebody acted up, they were blackballed from rodeo and we really tried to give rodeo a better reputation. Early on I hoped I'd have a grandson who could say rodeo is a good sport and my Grampa helped to make it so."

—Linder Diary, December, 1985

Rodeo in North America is a multi-million dollar business and one of the fastest growing sports, with nearly nine hundred sanctioned rodeos, and approximately eleven thousand cowboys vying for twenty-five million dollars in prize money.

One can attend a rodeo at the Cow Palace in San Francisco or the National Finals Rodeo (NFR) in Las Vegas; at the Williams Lake (British Columbia) Stampede, or the Canadian Finals in Edmonton, Alberta, or "The Greatest Outdoor Show On Earth" at Calgary, Alberta. The sport is not only growing — but thriving.

Rodeo is Spanish for Round-Up and was originally pronounced ro-day-o before becoming ro-dee-o in the American and Canadian Northwest. This public exhibition of cowboy skills is also called Stampede, Round-Up Days, Pioneer Days, Frontier Days or the National Finals.

Rodeo grew out of the North American cattle industry which had its start when Spanish Conquistadors imported Spanish cattle to Mexico early in the sixteenth century.

These rugged and rangy cattle quickly multiplied and huge herds were established by large landowners known as Dons. Many of these cattle found their way into Texas, which was a part of Mexico from 1821-36. It became an independent republic in 1836 and the twenty-eighth state of the USA in 1845.

"Maverick" or unbranded cattle ran wild and free and were there for the taking by men with a brand.

Mexican vaqueros (cowboys) followed the cattle north of the Rio Grande, worked for Texas ranches and may have staged the first rodeos which were more like fiestas with superb Mexican horsemanship and roping.

Chuck Walters, writing in the 1955 annual issue of *Rodeo Sports News* had this to say about rodeo:

"The golden days of the early cattle business are blended into folklore and history, providing one of the most colourful modern sports with its essential independence of changing times. Out of the cattle industry came stories and out of the stories came songs. Cowboys camped on the plains and in the hills and sang to the restless herds. For the cowboy belonged to a class of his own. His was the gaudiest, the loneliest, the most adventurous, the most monotonous profession in the world."

Walters recounts a newspaper article covering a rodeo contest at Deer Trail, Colorado July 4, 1869.

"All the cowpokes from the Mill Iron outfit were there, and everywhere the brands of the Camp Stool and Hashknife ranches were to be seen. The rules specified that 'the horses should be ridden with a slick saddle, which means that the saddle must be free from the roll usually tied across the horse, that the stirrups must not be tied under the horse, and that the rider must not wear spurs.'

"The horses were all outlaws fresh off the range, impossible to break. The boys were anxious to compete for the day money. A young cowpuncher named Will Goff, hardly past the downy-faced stage, was rarin' to go, and the record of the contest quotes him as saying he'd 'ride anything with hair on it.' The boys eared down a deceptively gentle-looking horse and here's how an anonymous correspondent described the action.

"Will Goff pulled off his coat, threw his suspenders aside, took a reef in his belt, and with one bound, landed on the bay's back. Swish! and his felt hat whistled through the air and caught the bronco across the side of the head. The pony pitched violently for fifty yards, making about three hundred revolutions to the minute.

"The bay quit spinning and started to run. Will Goff brought the animal back to the roar of the crowd."

But it fell to an Englishman with the romantic sounding name of Emilnie Gardenshire to make the ride of the day. Gardenshire was a Mill Iron cowboy. He drew Montana Blizzard, a fine bay with a Hashknife brand. The early rodeo journalist described the battle between man and beast.

"Gardenshire, rawhide whip in hand, crawled aboard cautiously, and, once firm in his seat, began to larrup the bay unmercifully. A sight followed which tickled the spectators hugely. The Englishman rode with hands free and kept plying his whip constantly. There was a frightful mix-up of cowboy and horse, but Gardenshire refused to be unseated. For fifteen minutes, the bay bucked, pawed, and jumped from side to side, then amid cheers, the mighty Blizzard succumbed, and Gardenshire rode him around the circle at a gentle lope."

The Englishman was awarded the title "Champion Bronco Buster of the Plains" and a suit of clothes for his magnificent performance.

Maybe a missing link in rodeo's history was produced in San Antonio, in 1877. John "Bet A Million" Gates, with a scheme to sell barbed wire, secured permission to erect an arena in the Military Plaza and advertised a cowboy exhibition.

He declared he would bring in wild Longhorn cattle and outlaw horses and pay prizes to the riders. A great crowd was drawn and Gates proved his point — that "bobwire" would hold the wildest livestock.

In 1882, prior to organizing his wild west show, Buffalo Bill persuaded North Platte, Nebraska businessmen to offer premiums for roping and bronco breaking contests. Thousands of handbills proclaiming an "Old Glory Blow Out" were distributed. Cody predicted a hundred competitors. Nearly a thousand showed up. Perhaps this was the first rodeo with too many entries.

Winfield, Kansas held a rodeo in 1882, while cash prizes were first given at a rodeo at Pecos City, Texas in 1883 when the boys from rival ranching outfits used the courthouse yard for a corral and worked off their frustrations in a steer roping contest.

For the first truly organized rodeo, Prescott, Arizona, July 4, 1888,

gets the nod. It was a commercial venture, a purse was put up and admission was charged.

The last full week in July, 1996 marked the ninety-ninth annual "Daddy of 'Em All". No other rodeo can top that. Even through both World Wars, Cheyenne (Wyoming) Frontier Days has not missed a single performance since the cannon was fired at high noon, September 23, 1897.

By virtue of being the longest, continually-held annual rodeo, Cheyenne Frontier Days is the USA's oldest organized rodeo.

That first Frontier Day program of "Wild Bronco Riding, Roping, Throwing and other Cowboy Feats" featured a purse of $100 for best pitching and bucking horse and $25 for best bronco rider.

First on the list of rules laid down by Cheyenne's original executive committee in 1897 was that: "In all contests where an entrance fee is charged, the entrance money will be added to the purse."

Rodeo Sports News says a rodeo attended by twelve thousand people was held in Denver, Colorado in September, 1887. Dr. Clifford Westermeier, author of *Man, Beast, Dust: The Story of Rodeo*, observed that Denver proved the future of cowboy sports ten years before Cheyenne's Frontier Days and a year before Prescott. Pendleton's Round-Up and Calgary's "fabulous" Stampede were not even a wistful look in a promoter's eye when Denver passed her bid to become the rodeo sports centre for all of North America.

In a book published by the Calgary Brewing and Malting Company Limited in 1971, the British writer Captain Mayne Reid, tells of a Round-Up June 10, 1847. His letter describes a "donneybrook" in the Mexican town of Santa Fe, New Mexico, with cowhands having a great time in roping and steer throwing events. During the night, there were celebrations and dances in the street.

Some say that rodeo had its start when a Round-Up ended and cowboys from three or four ranches matched brawn and skill with untamed range horses and wild steers. The wide open spaces formed the arena and the cowboys themselves were the spectators. Tequila or rye whiskey were refreshments and after a branding, "prairie oysters" (the testicles from young male calves) made up the menu.

The Calgary book, put together by members of the Foothills Cowboys'

Famous Alberta cowboys Dick Cosgrave, Clem Gardner, Herman Linder and Pete Knight in the Calgary Horseman's Hall of Fame. The figures were cast in wax and showed the cowboys visiting in a Calgary Stampede chuckwagon barn. The four were on display at the Calgary Brewery until being moved to the Glenbow Museum.

Linder Collection

Association, gives this chronology of the development of rodeo in North America:

"An exhibition of steer riding was held at Cheyenne, Wyoming in July, 1872, much to the annoyance of some townspeople who thought such an event was too vulgar to hold in a populated centre where the gritty language of the cowboys could easily be overheard.

"The first fully commercial rodeo was organized at Lander, Wyoming in 1893 by E. Farlow who made it a Frontier Days festival.

"Rodeo moved indoors for the first time at the Stockyards Coliseum in Fort Worth, Texas in 1917 and so became a year-round sport."

Ray Knight for whom the town of Raymond, Alberta was named. Linder Collection

Fred Kennedy, a Herman Linder rodeo publicist and Calgary Stampede historian, said there were lots of impromptu Sunday afternoon "rodeos." A so-called "un-rideable" horse would turn up among the wild ones at some district ranch and if the official horse-breaker couldn't stick to the outlaw, other riders would be invited to try their luck, for a side bet or two.

"There were few rules," said Kennedy. "A cowboy would climb aboard and ride a bronc to the finish. Later, someone suggested the idea of placing a silver dollar on the flat of each stirrup and if the coins were still in place

at the end of the ride, a new champion was born."

Canada's first formal rodeo was held July 1, 1902 at Raymond, Alberta — thirty miles southeast of the City of Lethbridge, a community with its own great rodeo heritage.

Raymond was named after Raymond Knight, son of an early Mormon settler (Jesse Knight) to the region. Knight started the Bar K2 Ranch which consisted of four hundred thousand acres of land, fenced and divided into many pastures and, stocked with fifteen thousand head of cattle, one thousand head of horses and forty thousand head of sheep. (At the close of the First World War, prices for land, livestock and commodities collapsed sharply and eventually Knight would lose all his assets.)

According to *Raymond Remembered*, a history of the Raymond community (published in 1993 to mark the town's ninetieth birthday), Knight suggested that cowboys from two surrounding ranches ought to compete against each other and he would provide the stock. Only two events were held out on a bleak and barren patch of prairie — calf roping and bronc riding.

Several cowboys showed up in 1902 for the big event, as did several

Ray Knight, right, with His Royal Highness the Prince of Wales.

It was not unusual for a large group of Maple Creek and district cowboys and ranchers to attend the Murraydale Stampede in the early part of the century. Seen with his horse and trophy after a local contest (front and centre) is the well-known Ed Keeley, who served in the army with the author's father in France in the First World War. From left: George Naismith, Lug LaValley, Bob Leslie, Cecil Stockdale, Mike Klaibert and Sam Cooper while the boy is Bob Doonan. Also seen: Percy Meggett, Gib O'Hare, Ed Birchall, Tom Buckingham and Fred Bradford. The men are standing outside the Birchall livery barn in Maple Creek which once covered half-a-block.

Picture courtesy Bob Doonan

hundred spectators. They surrounded much of the field with their carriages and democrats to view the spectacle. And, they were not disappointed. Ray Knight won the roping and Ed Corless, from the McCarty ranch, rode his bareback bucking horse to a standstill. Prizes for the contest were provided by Knight.

Lawrence Turner, editor of *Raymond Remembered*, recalls the Knight family providing one hundred and forty acres on the east edge of town, for the building of a race track, a grandstand and a stampede arena. This was completed in time for the stampede of July 1, 1903 a tradition which continues to this day.

Turner said the Raymond Stampede has been advertised as Canada's first stampede from day one.

Herman Linder competed at Raymond for several years and was always in the win column. For example, in 1934 he was first in bareback and first in calf roping and in his final year of riding in 1939 he was first in bareback. He also produced the Raymond Stampede for a number of years when it was a part of the Southern Alberta Rodeo circuit.

Stavely, Alberta is a cowtown located sixty miles south of Calgary on Number Two Highway. It has seen many race meets and stampedes, one of the first held about 1916 at the agricultural grounds — now the golf course.

Stavely made headlines in June, 1929 when Harry Streeter staged an indoor rodeo in the Stavely skating rink. This show, being the first of its kind in the country, drew the best and biggest name in rodeo at the time.

Pete Knight of Crossfield, Alberta.

Many young cowboys from Stavely, Nanton and Claresholm also competed and Sam (Sandy) Connell won the bronc riding and Pat Burton from Claresholm, the calf roping.

Stavely continues its rodeo tradition holding a professional rodeo in May of each year and an amateur rodeo in August.

There are a number of communities in Alberta and Saskatchewan which claim an early start to stampedes.

Chief among them is the Murraydale Picnic and Stampede which started in 1909 and is located twenty-five miles southeast of Maple Creek, Saskatchewan, which is known as "The Little Cow Town Of The West."

During the first years, the Murraydale bucking horses consisted of the farmers' and ranchers' horses that were driven to the picnic.

According to Ken Galbraith in *Ravenscrag, — Between and Beyond the Benches*, everything was free the first few years. Mr. Boardman made ice cream with a hand-turned freezer, then he rigged up a gas engine to turn the freezer. The women set up long tables to eat at, something like a potluck dinner.

"Sometime before 1920, corrals were built and bucking stock was brought in. Some years they used steers belonging to Pa Brown and horses belonging to Gib O'Hare. In the beginning, admission was twenty-five cents for ladies and gents. In 1934 it was thirty-five cents for adults and children under twelve were free; by 1953 it was one dollar.

"A cairn was built in 1971 in memory of the old timers, who started the picnic and kept it going. The plaque is kept in the Maple Creek Museum and taken

Bob Doonan is a pioneer of the Murraydale area.
Picture courtesy Bob Doonan.

to the Murraydale picnic grounds every year at stampede time."

Galbraith makes the claim the Murraydale Stampede and Picnic has grown to be the oldest continuous stampede in Western Canada.

George Willcocks in his recent book, *A History of Exhibitions and Stampedes in Medicine Hat*, claims the first record of a commercial stampede in Western Canada was one held in Medicine Hat, North West Territories in 1901.

He claims the main competitions were bareback riding and steer roping involving three- to five-year-old steers weighing up to fifteen hundred pounds. Doing the organizing and managing was a well-known local cowboy and rancher, Darias Allen. Among those assisting and participating were: Jack Hargrave, Jim Mitchell, Jim McLennan, Jim Fisher, A.C. Wiffen, J. Quesnell and Sol Boyer.

"In 1901, there was a steer roping contest but there was no fenced infield which resulted in steers often charging into the spectators or heading for the wide open prairies with the riders in hot pursuit. If a rider missed with his first attempt, he continued chasing the steer with second and third tries if necessary. This event was won by Michael Quesnell with a time of six minutes, forty seconds," says the Willcocks history.

Rodeo Association Of America Formed

"...Attended a meeting of the Rodeo Association of America and met many interesting people."

— Linder diary, January 21, 1940

There were no governing bodies and few, if any, hobbles on rodeo as a sport in the early years of the twentieth century. But animal activists were biding their time to bring rodeo to an abrupt and complete stop.

"Things erupted in 1929 in the State of California when the Humane Society went to court to outlaw the sport of rodeo with all kinds of allegations of cruelty to animals. This created a real ruckus and much negative publicity," Herman recalled.

This ballerina bull does a vertical nose dive while the luckless rider is horizontal with nose in the dirt. Is rodeo tough on animals? How about the cowboys?

Linder collection

Maxwell McNutt of Redwood City, California, a rodeo enthusiast and retired judge was alarmed at the threat to the sport he loved and sat down with neighbouring Salinas rodeo officials. They summoned help from rodeo management in faraway places: Calgary, Alberta (Guy Weadick); Pendleton, Oregon and Cheyenne, Wyoming. It was a case of all for one and one for all. If rodeo were to die in California, it would not go unscathed elsewhere.

Those in attendance formed the Rodeo Association of America and went to court and successfully defended rodeo contests. (The activists would come back to haunt rodeo in Vancouver, British Columbia, twenty years later.)

Charter president McNutt said the RAA was organized with the view of raising the quality of rodeos, protecting the interest and welfare of all involved, namely: the contestants, the animal, the organizations holding individual shows and the public, or as expressed in its constitution:

Wrote McNutt in the *RAA Bulletin* of May 5, 1937: "The purpose for which this association is formed is: To insure harmony among the rodeo associations in America and to perpetuate traditions connected with the livestock industry and cowboy sports incidental thereto; to standardize the same and adopt rules looking towards the holding of contests upon a uniform base; to minimize so far as practical, conflict in dates of contests; and to place such sports so nearly as may be possible on a par with amateur athletic events."

The Salinas rodeo, being located in the State of California, gave a little. They traded steer wrestling for steer decorating and the cowboy, instead of wrestling a steer to the ground, would slip an elastic band around the nose of the steer.

The Calgary Stampede had introduced steer decorating in 1927 and cowboys attempted to place a red ribbon over the horn of a steer while going at full gallop. Herman said these cattle were from the USA, weighed twelve to fourteen hundred pounds, and usually had a lot of Brahma blood in them. Smaller rodeos used Hereford or Highland cattle for the event. Steer wrestling returned to Calgary in 1967, three years after Herman had reintroduced the event in the Southern Alberta Rodeo Circuit.

1994 Canadian World Champions attend the Belt Buckle Awards of the Professional Rodeo Cowboys' Association at Colorado Springs, Colorado in early 1995. From left, are: Steer Wrestling Champion Blaine Pederson and wife Yvonne of Amisk, Alberta; Herman Linder and Bull Riding Champion Daryl Mills of Pink Mountain, British Columbia.   *HG Photo*

By 1938, the RAA could claim that nearly one hundred rodeos in the USA and Canada (two) belonged to their group.

As members of the RAA, each rodeo issued points to the winners, not only in the finals, but day monies, whose points went toward awarding the World's Championship in the various events and to the Grand Champion. One point was awarded for each dollar paid, including entrance fees added, in the roping, wrestling and decorating events and one and a half points for each dollar paid, including entrance fees added in the riding events. The contestant who, during the year, received the most points was declared the World's Champion Cowboy.

Some rodeos, like Boston Garden, did not join the RAA, while member Calgary Stampede ranked tenth in prize money ($6,127.50), and the Cardston Stampede offered winnings of $1,072.65.

Weadick would serve on the RAA board of directors in 1929 and

again from 1932-1934. His place was taken by E.L. Richardson, Calgary Stampede general manager, who would serve from 1935-1938.

Working relationships between the RAA and the Cowboys' Turtle Association (CTA) were not always amicable, but the sport managed to flourish with each passing year.

Things flowed along and the RAA sought commercial sponsors for prizes for annual cowboy champions. Heading the list was Levi-Strauss Company (overall manufacturers) of San Francisco who put up $500 cash for the Grand Champion Cowboy. Lesser amounts, usually in the $100 range, were provided to champions in other events.

Enter Lee Overalls, another manufacturer of rangemen's wear and their representative L.G. Baird. His company also wanted to put up prize money for RAA champions, "a lot more than $500," according to Herman. Their offer was turned down flat by the association with no reasons given.

Enraged with the RAA's refusal to better the lot of the cowboy, the late Bill Linderman of the Rodeo Cowboys Association (successor to the CTA), said the cowboys would look after their own rodeo points and prizes and cut all ties to the RAA.

Herman and later-day Champions at the Edmonton Rodeo.   *Cunningham Photo*

"Bill Linderman (later killed in an airplane crash at Salt Lake City,

The late Bill Linderman ... bright rodeo star and executive, lost in a Salt Lake City, Utah plane crash.   Linder Collection

enough on "Boxer"

Utah) was a good friend and I asked him to give the RAA one more year to change their thinking on prize money for the champions.

"He would have none of it," Herman recalled.

So the cowboys went their own way and the results can be seen in the successful National Finals Rodeo in Las Vegas, Nevada, each December and the Canadian Finals Rodeo in Edmonton, Alberta, each November.

As for the RAA, it eventually faded away without a whimper.

To the credit of President McNutt and his board of directors, their association possibly saved the sport of rodeo and gave it both structure and cohesiveness. The Boston strike might have been averted had that rodeo belonged to the RAA and watched overall management more closely. That didn't happen and it was the cowboys who eventually won the day.

Today, in Canada, major fairs belong to the Canadian Association of Fairs and Exhibitions (CAFE) and have contracts with the Canadian Rodeo Cowboys Association and individual stock contractors, where rodeo is concerned.

Rodeo is made up of the unusual and the spectacular. Above is Margie Greenough of Red Lodge, Montana on a saddle bronc. Below is Buddy Heaton of Kansas, riding a bareback horse at the Calgary Stampede without benefit of a surcingle.

Linder Collection

Original Turtle Documents
1936

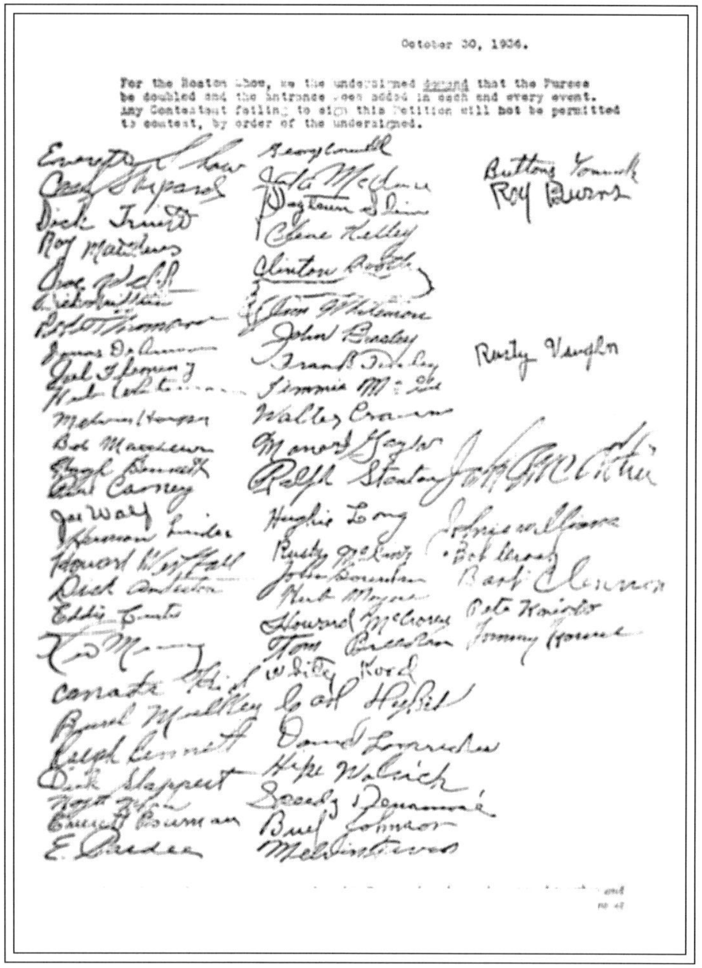

Above: Rusty McGinty President

At left: Eddie Woods Vice-President

Above: Hugh Bennett Secretary-Treasurer

At left: Everett Bowman Speaker

October 30, 1936.

For the Boston Show, we the undersigned demand that the Purses be doubled and the Entrance Fees added in each and every event. Any Contestant failing to sign this Petition will not be permitted to contest, by order of the undersigned.

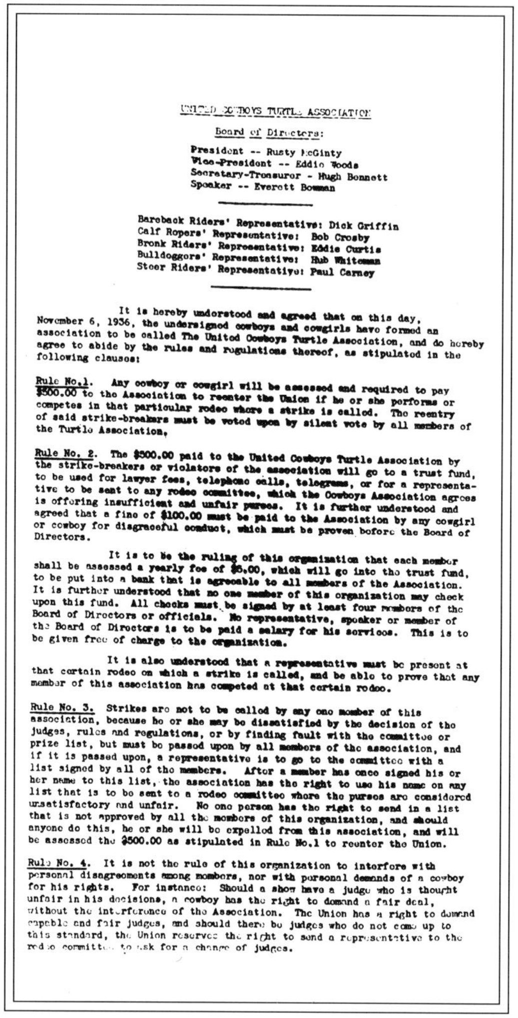

[document with numerous handwritten signatures]

UNITED COWBOYS TURTLE ASSOCIATION

Board of Directors:

President -- Rusty McGinty
Vice-President -- Eddie Woods
Secretary-Treasurer - Hugh Bennett
Speaker -- Everett Bowman

Bareback Riders' Representative: Dick Griffin
Calf Ropers' Representative: Bob Crosby
Bronk Riders' Representative: Eddie Curtis
Bulldoggers' Representative: Hub Whiteman
Steer Riders' Representative: Paul Carney

It is hereby understood and agreed that on this day, November 6, 1936, the undersigned cowboys and cowgirls have formed an association to be called The United Cowboys Turtle Association, and do hereby agree to abide by the rules and regulations thereof, as stipulated in the following clauses:

Rule No. 1. Any cowboy or cowgirl will be assessed and required to pay $500.00 to the Association to reenter the Union if he or she performs or competes in that particular rodeo where a strike is called. The reentry of said strike-breakers must be voted upon by silent vote by all members of the Turtle Association.

Rule No. 2. The $500.00 paid to the United Cowboys Turtle Association by the strike-breakers or violators of the association will go to a trust fund, to be used for lawyer fees, telephone calls, telegrams, or for a representative to be sent to any rodeo committee, which the Cowboys Association agrees is offering insufficient and unfair purses. It is further understood and agreed that a fine of $100.00 must be paid to the Association by any cowgirl or cowboy for disgraceful conduct, which must be proven before the Board of Directors.

It is to be the ruling of this organization that each member shall be assessed a yearly fee of $5.00, which will go into the trust fund, to be put into a bank that is agreeable to all members of the Association. It is further understood that no one member of this organization may check upon this fund. All checks must be signed by at least four members of the Board of Directors or officials. No representative, speaker or member of the Board of Directors is to be paid a salary for his services. This is to be given free of charge to the organization.

It is also understood that a representative must be present at that certain rodeo on which a strike is called, and be able to prove that any member of this association has competed at that certain rodeo.

Rule No. 3. Strikes are not to be called by any one member of this association, because he or she may be dissatisfied by the decision of the judges, rules and regulations, or by finding fault with the committee or prize list, but must be passed upon by all members of the association, and if it is passed upon, a representative is to go to the committee with a list signed by all of the members. After a member has once signed his or her name to this list, the association has the right to use his name on any list that is to be sent to a rodeo committee where the purses are considered unsatisfactory and unfair. No one person has the right to send in a list that is not approved by all the members of this organization, and should anyone do this, he or she will be expelled from this association, and will be assessed the $500.00 as stipulated in Rule No. 1 to reenter the Union.

Rule No. 4. It is not the rule of this organization to interfere with personal disagreements among members, nor with personal demands of a cowboy for his rights. For instance: Should a show have a judge who is thought unfair in his decisions, a cowboy has the right to demand a fair deal, without the interference of the Association. The Union has a right to demand capable and fair judges, and should there be judges who do not come up to this standard, the Union reserves the right to send a representative to the rodeo committee to ask for a change of judges.

18

Cowboys' Turtle Association Paved The Way For ProRodeo

"... We were having meetings all day trying to get things straightened out. We went to the rodeo and booed. Finally got old Colonel to make agreement and sign."

-Linder diary, November 2, 1936

In the fall of 1936, sixty-one unhappy and restless rodeo cowboys decided to band together for their own common good and the welfare of a sport in need of rules, regulations and reform.

Professional rodeo in North America would hardly be what it is today were it not for the contestants who went on strike in Boston Garden, November 3, 1936.

And Canada's Herman Linder was one of those at the centre of the storm.

Herman said that, without a doubt, the big issue at Boston was the smallness of the prize money offered. The cowboys wanted their entry fees added to the purse and they also wanted the prize money to be increased by $4,000. The show was attracting huge crowds and they felt the performers should have a bigger share of the profits.

"Take Hugh Bennett, for instance," said Herman. "He was one of the top money winners in the USA. He travelled all the way from his ranch in Arizona to attend the Boston show, won two championship events, yet he cleared only $350."

Writing in *Persimmon Hill*, magazine of the National Cowboy Hall of Fame and Western Heritage Center, the late Gene Pruett said that the Boston purse for ten days was such that the top man in any event would win barely enough to cover his expenses. The purse was increased, but if that had been all, the whole incident would have been unimportant. The main fact was that the protesting cowboys came through a trying experience with the knowledge that they had rights as individuals, and by agreement among themselves could stand up for those rights.

Pruett said it took courage for that small group of cowboys at Boston in 1936 to say: "We want." They had never won before, and they had no real reason to believe they would win this time; and losing might have

barred them from a sport at which even then they were depending upon for a livelihood. They won — but the newspaper stories do not tell of the all-night sessions. Talking brave, but feeling scared. Staking everything on the belief that they were right.

The cowboy petition read: "For the Boston show, we the undersigned demand that the Purses be doubled and the Entrance Fees added in each and every event. Any Contestant failing to sign this Petition will not be permitted to contest, by order of the undersigned."

The show's promoter, the wily Colonel W. T. Johnson, thought differently and reacted in typical fashion. He decided he would just ignore the loss of sixty-one top competitors and put on the show with those he had on contract and a wide assortment of pick-up men and stable hands.

The Colonel directed the rodeos at both Madison Square Garden in New York City and the Boston Garden. He would furnish stock at a $100,000 contract for New York and $80,000 for Boston. He was one of the nation's most famous rodeo producers. His Bird Nest Ranch in Texas covered twenty-five thousand acres and he would ship as many as nine hundred head of livestock to New York and Boston for those east coast rodeos.

Johnson's public relations pamphlets called him the "angel of rodeo."

"He was an honest-to-goodness showman and he had great bucking stock," said Herman.

What Johnson didn't advertise was that the Boston rodeo, which followed on the heels of the New York show (more than $30,000 in prize money), offered a lot less in winnings for the cowboys.

He was outraged with cowboy demands asking that the purses be doubled and the entrance fees added in every event. "Before I give in to anything so ridiculous I'll sink all my stock in the bay," he shouted.

He was noted for his slick, colourful, fast-paced rodeos, had a stubborn streak a mile long and was not overly-generous to cowboy entrants.

"We are going to put on a first-class rodeo, just as good as ever has been staged in Boston," Colonel Johnson declared after the top hands left. "We have plenty of cowboys now enroute from Chicago where they just finished up a rodeo."

He sent a telegram to Chicago, where another rodeo was being held, and offered contestants $500 each to travel to Boston and break the strike.

But Herman says the strikers had received assurances in writing from the one hundred and thirty to one hundred and thirty-five contestants in the Chicago show that they had no intention of coming to Boston as strikebreaking cowboys. The riders could see there was a big issue at stake and they decided to let things unwind in their own time and in their own way.

According to Kris Fredriksson, rodeo authority and curator of history at Texas Tech University at Lubbock in *Pro Rodeo Sports News*: "For the first time, the cowboys had jointly voiced the complaints which had been building up for a number of years. The cowboys merely wanted to make a decent living in a fair contest. A contestant's average income in 1935 (the year before Boston) was $2,000; in 1937 (the year after Boston), $3,000."

This was not the first time cowboys fussed about poor pay.

The curator said that much earlier, *The Fort Worth Gazette* reported in March, 1883, "three hundred and twenty-five cowboys from several ranches in the Texas Panhandle waged a successful strike, resulting in wages increasing from $1.18 to $1.68 per day." But rodeo contestants they were not!

Noted Willard H. Porter, writing in *The Western Horseman* (September, 1986): "In 1915, Homer S. Wilson and Fay Ward collaborated to form 'The Wild Bunch,' whose official, though cumbersome, title was The Wild Bunch Contest Fair and Roundup Association. The idea was sound, but before its time, and the group soon faded."

Here's how Boston's newspapers of 1936 told the story:

Roper Hugh Bennett, right, with Herman at Pike's Peak Rodeo, August 12, 1989.
Linder Collection

RODEO OPENS MINUS STARS

"The World Championship rodeo opened at Boston Garden last night without the world champions — they were all out on strike. They had refused to risk their necks in the various events unless Col. W.T. Johnson, producer of the show, would meet their demands for more prize money. Some sixty-one of the best riders in the country walked out.

STARS WHO QUIT

"Hugh Bennett, one of the biggest rodeo attractions in the country, and a leader in the strike, comes from Arizona. He's a college graduate, and owner of his own ranch.

"Among the other top hands leaving are such headliners as Hub Whiteman, Texas, winner of the 1935 Bulldogging championship; Everett

Shaw, this year's world champion Calf Roper; Jack McClure, New Mexico; Eddie Curtis, Oklahoma, world champion Bronco Rider; Dick Truitt, Oklahoma; E. Padre, Colorado, winner of Calf Roping championships in Pendleton, Cheyenne, and Madison Square Garden.

"Included are such famed riders as Everett Bowman, Rusty McGinty, Herman Linder, Dick Griffith, Dogtown Slim, Walter Cravens, Leo Murray, Joe Fleming, Pete Knight, Eddie Wood, Ralph Bennett, Jackie Cooper, Joe Welch, Joe Wolf, Manerd Gaylor, Jim Whiteman, Roy Matthews, Hoytt Hefner, Jim McGee, Melvin Harper, Bob Crosby, Luther McGinty, Bart Clennon and others."

Prior to the opening of the rodeo at the Garden, the lobby of the Hotel Manager was the scene of an indignation meeting, after the cowboys had stabled their horses in nearby livery stables and prepared for the long trek homewards. All planned to stay over for the opening performance to see what kind of a show would be put on, then leave the next morning.

And, said Herman, "here's where things got downright interesting."

Prior to the evening's performance, the strikers had one of their number dress up in ordinary city clothes, venture to the box office and pick up a batch of tickets. It was the first time these champions had ever watched rodeo from the public stands. In silence they waited for the final announcement which signalled the start of the Grand Entry. The time for the introduction of their antagonist, Colonel Johnson.

Calgary author Cliff Faulknor, with his early book on Herman Linder, Turn Him Loose, and the children's book, White Calf. HG Photo

In his book, *Turn Him Loose, (Herman Linder, Canada's Mr. Rodeo)* Calgary, Alberta author, Cliff Faulknor, describes what happened next:

"As Johnson came riding forward to the centre of the arena, the sixty-one waiting cowboys let out such an outcry of shouting and booing the announcer's voice was drowned in the din. The band suddenly launched into *The Star Spangled Banner*, which brought the cowboys to their feet out of respect for the anthem and delayed the demonstration for a few minutes. But the band couldn't go on saluting Old Glory forever. Then, under the strain, the band leader must have temporarily lost his sanity or control for he led his crew into a brilliant rendition of *Empty Saddles In The Old Corral*.

"This was too much for the cowboys who immediately joined in, bellowing the words lustily. Amid great laughter, the delighted crowd accompanied them, filling the cavernous arena with a screaming bedlam of sound. Now in utter confusion, the band hastily switched to a less appropriate tune, but the damage was done.

"For a moment an uneasy quiet reigned, then the announcer called the bronc riding events and the strikers started booing again.

"Except for an occasional shout of 'Bring On The Cowboys' and 'When Are You Going To Show Us Some Riders', the strikers watched in grim amusement while stable hands, chute men and roustabouts, who had never seriously competed for prize money, came thundering into the arena uneasily perched on heaving broncs. For good measure, Colonel Johnson threw in Wild West actors and pick-up men. Rider after rider was promptly bucked off, or failed to make a qualified ride. The spectators grew disgusted and called to see some riders.

"Colonel Johnson knew he was beaten and called striker spokesman Everett Bowman over to him and agreed to meet all their demands"

Here's how the Boston press reported things the next day:

COWBOYS WIN RODEO STRIKE

"Prize Money Increased. Engaging in the first big strike in the long history of rodeo, sixty-one cowboys — watched Colonel W.T. Johnson's opening contest from the stands at Boston Garden last night — and got paid for it.

"After intermediaries had held frequent conferences with the Colonel an agreement was finally reached, and the champions will be back in the contest starting tonight.

"The cowboys won every one of their points. In addition, as a bonus of goodwill, the management of the Garden saw to it that all the cowboys who paid money to watch the events would be given $20 as goodwill money ... ten times what they had paid to get in to see the show!

"At times, the cowboys made such a wild demonstration that the rodeo nearly was stopped. Police repeatedly warned them, and once came close to clearing the section.

"The saddle bronc event in which grooms from the stable, chute men and others who never were in the real prize money did the riding, brought down a wild din of wailing and booing. Rider after rider bucked off or failed to make a ride.

"The rodeo was a failure that night and Garden officials told patrons to keep their ticket stubs and to come back the next night.

"Finally at eleven o'clock, the Colonel signed an agreement giving the top hands an additional $4,000 in prize money to make a total for fourteen performances stand at about $14,000. He also agreed to restore the entry fee which each cowboy must pay before he can sign up for a contest.

"Terms agreed upon tonight bring the prize money at Boston to a figure to be compared with the other large rodeos," Dick Truitt, spokesman for the steer wrestlers, said.

"Herman Linder, one of the greatest bronc-stompers who ever rode down an 'outlaw' represented the bronc riders in the dealings with the Colonel. He made it clear that the argument was directed at what he called 'a fair share of the prize money.'

"None of the intermediaries — Linder, Truitt, Hugh Bennett and Dick Griffith — sought to embarrass the Garden. Their claim was based on the fact that only seven 'day moneys' were to be paid for fourteen contests and at a standard lower than was necessary.

"Colonel Johnson said, 'I don't hold any hard feelings against the men; they have to earn their living by winning prize money. But sometimes they don't appreciate the difficulties of managing a rodeo.'" It would be the last rodeo he would stage.

In his autobiography, *Horseman, Brand of a Legend*, the late Hugh L. Bennett, first (and longtime) secretary-treasurer of the Turtles, said Johnson sold out the night of the strike to Gene Autry, the Clemens Brothers from Arizona and Everett Colburn from Texas.

"We never did see the Colonel any more. He meant what he said. He wasn't going to be dictated to. I feel awful proud to have started the association. There wasn't any way that his snow job could go on, for there wasn't anyone making any money except old man Johnson."

It wasn't only the cowboys who were happy Boston ended on a happy note. Garden manager George Brown said: "I am extremely pleased at the outcome of the strike, for it means Boston will be able to see the best cowboys in the world competing in real contests." In that one evening, manager Brown had apparently seen enough poor riders to last him a lifetime.

The first executive of the Turtles included Rusty McGinty, president; Eddie Woods, vice-president; Hugh Bennett, secretary-treasurer; Everett Bowman, spokesman; and representatives Bob Crosby, Eddie Curtis, Dick Griffith, Hub Whiteman and Paul Carney.

CTA officers for 1937 included Bowman, president (he would hold the office for eight years); Linder, first vice-president; McGinty, second vice-president; and Bennett, secretary-treasurer.

When the early days of the Turtles is reviewed, some names are frequently mentioned: Bowman, Bennett, Linder, McGinty, Woods, Everett Shaw, Burel Mulkey and Hughie Long.

Bowman and Bennett were married to twin sisters. Josie Bennett and Lois Bowman helped to collect new fees, picked up annual dues and supported the CTA in many ways.

Mrs. Hugh (Josie) Bennett was the CTA's first secretary, keeping the books from the back seat of her husband's car or truck. There was no office nor pay of any kind.

Recalled Porter in *The Western Horseman*:

"It is extraordinary to reveal that in 1945, when the CTA became the Rodeo Cowboys Association, an audit was taken by the new (and first) business manager, Earl Lindsey, and it was discovered that the books 'were off' by only a few pennies. The audit went back to 1937 and included the

The Boston Garden strike ended on a happy note and Herman Linder, third from left, representing the bronc riders presents a clock and pen set to Garden manager George Brown, third from right, who did not approve of the treatment given to cowboys by Col. W.T. Johnson, rodeo producer/manager. Watching the presentation from left are: Everett Bowman, Hugh Bennett, unidentified and Leo Murray.   Linder Collection

Josie Bennett/Lois Bowman years, plus the years that the first paid secretary, Fanny Lovelady, was in charge, commencing in 1939 with an office in Phoenix."

Bart Clennon, 85, who also competed at Boston, said money wasn't the only thing sticking in the cowboys' craw.

"We wanted fair judging, there was out and out favouritism at some rodeos and we wanted it stopped," he said.

Herman agreed. "Pendleton and Cheyenne were some of the worst in a lot of ways. They had great rodeos, but then they'd get somebody from a store with a big car and a big hat and use him as a judge. He didn't have to know anything about rodeo.

As reported in *ProRodeo Sports News*, cowboys weren't without their sins either. "A lot of guys (cowboys) were beating hotel bills and writing bad cheques," Clennon said. "We wanted to straighten that out."

The News said it took some time, but the cowboys did straighten out a lot of problems. In fact The Boston cowboys were about to take part in the greatest revolution ever to shake the world of rodeo.

Reported *The News*: "The World Championship rodeo at Boston Garden ended November 11, 1936 after its required ten-day stint. But the world of rodeo had changed forever."

There followed many minor incidents, but none so severe as the Boston episode occurred again — not because there haven't been difficulties, disputes and differences, but

Herman, left, and Bart Clennon of Tucson, Arizona were two of sixty-one cowboys who signed the Cowboys' Turtle Association petition at Boston Garden in 1936 — forcing a one-day rodeo strike. They are the last survivors of that important event when rodeo came of age. Clennon competed in saddle bronc for nearly twenty years, won the bronc riding at Madison Square Garden, New York City in 1945 and was world's runner-up saddle bronc rider in 1951. This picture was taken at the Cowboy Reunion in Las Vegas, Nevada in 1995, sponsored by the Rodeo Historical Society.
HG Photo

because the contestants finally had representatives to carry their complaints to the offending parties. The contestant no longer stood alone. He was a "Turtle."

The CTA was not a large outfit. There were only twenty-five paying dues at the start. But as the months sped by, word got around the Turtles were on the right track and memberships came in steadily. Dues were five dollars and were to be used to finance necessary business such as talking with management or rodeo producers when differences surfaced. The longest serving president was Everett Bowman of Hillside, Arizona.

Turtle directors and members would often recount the kinds of things that provoked the Boston strike and the birth of their association.

Said Linder: "The organization helped the cowboys tremendously. The young men starting out the last two or three generations have no idea what they've got to help them in competition compared to what we had. For instance, in those early days we had ten rodeo chutes at Madison Square Garden and each saddle had a number on it. If your horse was in chute five you rode the saddle marked five. And it was the same with the bareback rigging. In those days, you might go to New York and never ride the same saddle twice. If you used resin, you were disqualified."

Bowman of Hillside, Arizona, now deceased, was acclaimed by Turtle members for his long years of service to the CTA. He could be stubborn and might not always be right, but if he thought he was right, he hung in 'til the end. And he stood for helping rodeo. By the time of the Boston affair in 1936, he had been rodeoing for fifteen years, and knew that the years it would take to really establish rodeo would do little to benefit him personally.

Newspapers all over North America had editorial comment on the strike. Said one Boston paper: "All the world champion bronco busters joined the labour movement last night, declared a strike, won it and announced they would go back to work in tonight's show."

Said *The Calgary Herald* of June 12, 1937: "Is rodeo going revolutionary? Instead of the free and easy men who follow the lure of every trail that promises bucking horses and wild steers for the wrangling, are we to have a group arguing for advantages long ignored? ... Have we passed the time when cowboys will want to present a swift-moving pageant of riding and roping for their own amusement and that of any onlookers who happen by?"

The writer concluded that the old free days were indeed passing and that it was time the rodeo rider had a fair shake. "Some of the largest crowds gather in places where the day money is far too small. These men, travelling distances from place to place, have heavy expenses, run big risks, and take chances on re-rides. The sum of a season's earnings for a man in the money looks far from generous when everything has been met. It had taken the man with the saddle and chaps a long time to discover that, if a remedy is to be found, he is the one to find it. And for this reason we have the newly-formed cowboy union which has been humorously styled, the Cowboys' Turtle Association.

By 1938, the Turtles had succeeded in establishing rules protecting their membership, rodeo committees and the general public. That year, their Articles of Association were distributed in printed form.

Strict Rules

The Cowboys' Turtle Association were not easy on contestants who gave rodeo a bad name.

Here's a few of their regulations in 1939, taken from the *Rodeo Association of America Bulletin* of that year:

"Any member who shows himself financially irresponsible, that is, who passed bad checks or fails to pay his board or hotel bill during the period of a given rodeo, shall be subject to a fine, suspension or both. (Members must obtain and keep receipts when bills have been paid.)

"If the board sees fit, it may advance payment for outstanding bills incurred by members during a given rodeo."

The following letters were published in the June, 1938 issue of the *Rodeo Association of America Bulletin*:

Fred S. McCargar
Secretary
RAA
Salinas, California

May 3, 1938

In the general rules of the RAA section nine, it is stated that any contestant may be barred from any show, and his money not refunded, for being under the influence of liquor. What I want to know is what can be done, with a judge, flagman or any arena official, if they are under the influence of liquor, when trying to judge or flag?

Let me know what you think about this as it is a very common thing to see the judges and timers drinking around the show.

Sincerely,

Everett Shaw
Cowboys' Turtle Association
Stonewall, Oklahoma

Mr. Everett Shaw
Stonewall, Oklahoma

May 14, 1938

Answering your letter of May 3, in which you ask what should be done with judges who get drunk. I agree with you that there should not be any difference between judges and contestants; in fact, there really should be a higher standard for judges than contestants. That is the reason why there is a clause in the rules whereby a judge can be protested and, if found guilty, can be barred from further judging.

Sincerely yours,

Fred S. McCargar
Secretary, RAA

The town of Cardston is nestled in the rolling foothills of southwest Alberta, just thirty minutes from the majesty of Waterton/Glacier International Peace Park. Here, in the shadows of the mountains, Cardston was established in 1887 by Mormon pioneers coming to Canada from Utah. This was one of the century's last great covered wagon migrations. While still residing in little mud-chinked log houses, and barely able to eke out an existence, these settlers started to build a temple. The Alberta Temple was opened in 1923 after ten years of construction and became the centrepiece of the town. It was the first temple constructed by the church outside of the continental U.S. Its architects, Hyrum Pope and Harold Burton, were strongly influenced by the work of Frank Lloyd Wright, which shows in the unique appearance of the massive granite structure. HG Photo

Herman Linder, Sr. and wife Marie in later years.

The Cahoon Hotel is still a Cardston landmark.

HG Photo

Residence of the Linder family. It later burned down. The senior Linders got their first radio in 1925.

The Start Of A Legend

From 1929 to 1939 the name Herman Linder blazed like a meteor across the rodeo world on three continents.

Starting with his hometown rodeo at Cardston, Alberta, he went on to worldwide acclaim and to win an unparalleled twenty-two championships at the famous Calgary Stampede — a record never equalled.

When he retired at the age of thirty-two after a big win in Lewiston, Idaho, he became a producer of rodeos and his name became synonymous with the sport in Canada. Rodeo has changed greatly over the past seventy years, and changed for the better. A strong factor in that change was the Cardston cowboy, Herman Linder.

It was a tearful farewell at the train station in Stockton, Illinois that day in 1918 when relatives and friends said goodbye to the Herman Linder Sr. family who were departing for the Canadian northwest and the southern corner of Alberta.

There was the senior Linder, mother Marie, daughters Minnie and Leona and sons Warner and Herman Jr.

The senior Linder had earlier emigrated from Switzerland where he had been an acrobat and tightrope artist. He grew tired of touring Europe with a travelling circus and with his wife, came to the United States where his older brother was established in Wisconsin.

Herman Jr. was born in Darlington, Lafayette County, Wisconsin, August 5, 1907. The Linders moved about twenty miles across the state line to Stockton, where Herman's dad set up in the cheese-making business.

It was a time when the Canadian Pacific Railway was advertising for people to come to the Canadian west where land was cheaper. The family landed in Cardston in the spring of 1918 and purchased a section of land, about six miles south of town, not far from the U.S. border.

The young brothers, Warner and Herman, lay in their beds at the Cahoon Hotel those first few nights, listening to the creak of wagons and the sound of horse's hooves. It was music to their ears.

Life was not easy on the Alberta plains. Herman recalls the drought years of 1918 and 1919 when hay jumped to $50 per ton. His father was going broke from the drought and then there was the blizzard of May, 1920 which claimed thousands of head of sheep and cattle — wiping out many a stockman. The Linders would sell a half section of their land to survive and kept the remaining land with buildings which would later form the core of a sixteen hundred acre spread.

What makes a champion cowboy?

Herman says he doesn't know, but he figures a bronc rider is born, not made. Herman and Warner loved to ride. They started riding yearling steers and wild range horses when they were teenagers.

Herman's first competitive ride was in 1924. In 1929, with a rough, tough five-year apprenticeship behind him he entered Calgary, and rode against Pete Knight, Earl Thode, Lee (Canada Kid) Ferris, Dan Utley and the Watrin boys. He emerged a hero — a winner of both the Canadian bronc riding championship with saddle and the open bareback bronc riding championship. By the end of 1939 he had won twenty-two titles at Calgary, a record that is unsurpassed, and probably never will be broken. He was crowned All-Around champion of Canada seven times, while competing

Herman and Agnes stand beside their log cabin, which was home to them for the first seven years of their marriage.
Glenbow Archives NA3253-4

on saddle and bareback broncs, steer decorating, steer riding and calf roping. He also won the North American All-Around five times.

His biggest thrill came when he "won it all" at the Calgary Stampede in 1934. He won first on bareback, first on bulls, first on saddle broncs (Canadian entries) and second on saddle broncs (open entries). He was also judged North American and Canadian All-Around Cowboy.

Herman's life story, his rise to rodeo stardom, the struggles of the Cowboys' Turtle Association (forerunner of today's Professional Rodeo Cowboys Association of which Linder is a life member) were chronicled in the book, *Turn Him Loose! Herman Linder, Canada's Mr. Cowboy*, by Cliff Faulknor in 1977.

Herman married Agnes Zeller, daughter of George and Rozina. She was born August 13, 1908 at Java, South Dakota and received her elementary training at Java and her normal school training at Aberdeen. She taught school in the Java area until her marriage to Herman, December 25, 1932. They were married fifty-two years prior to her death April 27, 1985. Her unfailing support to her husband and devotion to her family were an example to all.

Herman and son, George, at a Maine-Anjou cattle sale.
Alberta Beef Photo.

Herman says he and Agnes lived in a small cabin on the Linder ranch (some of their happiest days), from 1932 to 1939. "Mom and Dad lived in a two-room shack and we lived in the log cabin. I don't know how old it is, but it was old when my folks moved here in 1918.

"I went to Grade Eight and Nine in that log cabin, as well as the Lutheran Church. The cabin was bought from an outlaw originally — so it has seen everything: school and church, good and bad," he says.

The cabin remains on the ranch, tucked away in the yard — a reminder of tougher times and the better days that were to come.

"If my folks had their wish they couldn't have wished for anything that's half as good as we have now — water in the corrals, electricity, gas, radio and TV, cars and trucks."

Son George was born June 18, 1942 and died of heart failure while feeding cattle in the field January 5, 1986. He left a wife, Kia, and three daughters.

George had taken a strong interest in both cattle and farming operations and the Linders ran a feedlot and commercial beef finishing operation until 1969 when they were among the first Canadians to import Maine-Anjou beef cattle from France.

George was president of the Canadian Maine-Anjou Association in

A Linder Grand Champion bull at the Lethbridge Rocky Mountain Livestock Show, 1981.
Walt Browarny Photographics

LinderHaven Maine-Anjou at Poplar Haven Maine-Anjou, Wimborne, Alberta.
Walt Browarny Photographics

Herman has had a close and cordial cattle operation with the Smith brothers, Ron, Robert and Gary of Wimborne, Alberta.
Alberta Beef Photo

Mexican cattlemen honoured Alberta cattle breeders Herman Linder and Dick Fisher, right, with these scrolls. In the centre is Tony Saretsky, former manager of the Alberta Canada All Breeds Association.
Alberta Beef Photo

1974 and Herman president of the Alberta association in 1973-1974 and honourary chairman of the Maine-Anjou World Congress in Calgary in 1984.

Following the deaths of his wife and son, Herman moved his purebred cows to Poplar Haven Ranch (the Smith Brothers) at Wimborne, Alberta. Cattle from that herd are shown under the LinderHaven name.

A daughter, Rosemarie, was born June 18, 1944. A champion barrel racer, she married Tom Bews of Longview, Alberta in 1967. He is a five-time All-Around Canadian champion cowboy and commercial rancher. He and son Guy do considerable movie work (Lonesome Dove was one project). Both Guy and older brother TJ became involved in rodeo, TJ as a saddle bronc rider and Guy as steer wrestler. There are two more sons, Dusty and Peter.

Five years after the death of his first wife, Herman married Adeline Tellesch of Cut Bank, Montana on May 26, 1990. They reside on the ranch at Cardston when they're not spending holidays visiting friends or as rodeo spectators in village, town or city.

Tom and Rosemarie Bews and sons Guy, TJ, Dusty and Peter.
Linder Collection

Herman and Adeline (Tellesch) Linder with friend Meggie.
Linder Collection

Herman would go on to greater things ...
Glenbow Archives photo NA3252-5

Herman chummed with school pal Valmer Bates and, later on, complained to him how sore his back was from the saddle bronc ride. Valmer offered to put some Sloan's Liniment (an early cure-all for aches and pains which possessed a great sting) on Herman's back. Mischievously, he allowed some of that liniment to run down the crease of Herman's lower cheeks.

"You didn't want to be too close to Herman when that happened," Valmer said.

Herman laughs about it now, but he wasn't laughing then.

A Green Kid And A Green Horse

Herman Linder was just a green kid of twelve years when a threshing crew gave him the opportunity of making a dollar by riding a bareback horse on the wide-open prairie.

"A few of the fellows knew I was riding steers and horses at home so they dared me to ride a frisky horse that was hitched to a bundle wagon. They threw on an old-fashioned saddle with a big saddle horn and I was on in a flash and did that old horse give me the what-for. There were lots of times the men could see daylight between that horse's back and my backside, and sometimes I had both feet straight up in the air. But I hung on and rode him to a stop."

This is the Cardston "Over The Hill Gang" who love to test their cribbage hands against one another. From left: Valmer Bates, eighty-seven years young; Harry Scott, eighty-eight; and Herman, age eighty-nine. They're boyhood friends who have lots of stories to tell — if one has the time to listen.
HG Photo

"Alberta Pearl" Was No "Girl"

There was fun to spare and a good-natured crowd to boot that summer day in Cardston in 1921 when rodeo patrons saw their first "cowgirl" in action.

Fourteen-year-old Herman Linder had been offered six dollars by the rodeo committee to dress up as a girl and ride a bareback horse. Herman had been making quite a name for himself by riding steers and bucking horses at the Linder ranch.

So Herman was dressed in a floppy hat — tied under the chin with a pretty red ribbon — faded middy and a short skirt hidden by big, sheepskin chaps.

Cowboy let 'er buck! And Herman rode the sunfishing horse from one end of the arena to the other, and was finally scooped up by pick-up man Dud Leavitt, who took "Alberta Pearl" in front of the grandstand crowd. Every time Leavitt swung his horse about to show off the young rider, "Alberta Pearl" would face the other way.

Embarrassed beyond measure, Herman finally made his way back behind the chutes where he doffed his feminine attire and was once again all boy.

Sixteen-year-old Herman on a bareback in the Linder pasture.

Linder Collection

In the corral at home.

HG Photo

Herman Is A Homebody At Heart

Whether tending his lawn and flowers in retirement or feeding cattle in the snows of winter, Herman Linder was never a slacker.

At the age of twelve he drove a food and bedroll wagon on a sheep drive that extended one hundred and fifty miles, from Cardston, northeast to the British Block (Suffield, Alberta), some thirty miles from Medicine Hat.

Two local sheepmen sought better summer grazing for their herds and two wagons accompanied them, the second driven by fourteen-year-old Rex Harker, son of one of the owners.

Herman was homesick at the start, but he toughed things out over the next two months and came home a sun-bronzed veteran. Eight years later, Herman was looking forward to his twentieth birthday when he decided to leave home and go to work for someone else.

Sister Minnie (now Mrs. Fred Ingram), was living in Cutbank, Montana and had written about a possible job her brother could fill. The job didn't pan out so Herman hopped a freight that was heading west and for God knows where.

It was a dull day and the empty freight car he occupied was rather dark inside. Stretching out at the end of the car, sharp tingles played along his spine when a deep voice boomed from the other end, inquiring as to who Herman was and where was he headed.

Mindful he had a few dollars in his pocket, Herman had no intention of letting this rough-sounding stranger get the best of him and his wallet.

"I'm just out of jail for armed robbery," said Herman in the toughest possible voice.

Nothing else was said, but the stranger departed at the next siding.

The train lumbered along to Spokane, Washington where Herman joined the United States army. He quickly realized that footslogging was not his style and departed before the month was out. He spent the winter of 1926-27 on a Great Northern Railway construction crew and earned seventy-five dollars a month.

Then it was back home to Cardston and to the range and the horses he had grown to love so well.

Herman riding the Saddle Bronc, Cigarette, at the Calgary Stampede.
Linder Collection

Hell Bent For Leather

Friends can be a great asset in life and that's one of the reasons Herman Linder values them so highly.

It was two Cardston men who saw that he entered the Calgary Stampede in 1925 in the boys' steer riding; it was two cowboy contestants who told Herman he needed a different saddle to ride broncs well and it was good pal E.W. (Ted) Hinman who put up part of the money to buy the saddle at a rodeo in Milk River, Alberta in 1928.

Herman rode in his first stampede as "Alberta Pearl" at Cardston at the age of fourteen and was paid mount money of $6.

At the age of sixteen, he split first prize of $35 in saddle bronc riding, again at the Cardston Stampede, competing against a seasoned rodeo hand. The horse he rode that day was Yellow Fever, one of the toughest broncs of the day.

It was common knowledge in the Cardston ranching community that Herman and brother Warner spent a lot of time riding steers and broncs

Herman likes nice flowers and a tidy yard.

HG Photo

34

at the Linder ranch six miles south of town. So when it came time for the 1925 Calgary Stampede, it was rancher Ed Burton who put up the money for boys' steer riding entry fees and it was another rancher, Freeman Cook, who asked Herman to join his family for the Calgary trip.

Herman split second and third in the steer contest, losing out to W. Goodrich of Calgary, whose name was short-lived in rodeo circles. Herman won $5.50 in prize money and would return to Calgary four years later and claim the Canadian saddle bronc and bareback titles and prize money of $898.75. His total earnings at the "Greatest Outdoor Show on Earth" would equal $4,473.76 in the period 1925 to 1942 — an amount a contestant can earn in short order today.

Ted Hinman was teaching school in the Cardston area and boarding at the Linder ranch. He would later serve as Provincial Secretary in the government of Premier Ernest Manning.

Hinman had just bought a new Model A Ford equipped with a gear shift and was eager to try it out. It was July, 1928 and he decided to give his car a road test and was leaving for the Raymond Stampede fifty miles down the road. He was also a budding jockey and hoped to make a few dollars in the races. Herman joined him and took his Visalia saddle along.

Herman won third in the saddle bronc riding and Hinman won a couple of races. They decided to head over to Milk River where a stampede was being held the next day.

Contestants with the Alberta Stampede Company's show in Toronto in 1926 included, from left: Cowgirl Cross, Jack Cooper, "Slim" Pelley, Pete Knight, Joe Fisher, Pete Vandermeer, Barney Hogg, Herb Matier and Jim Carey. Fisher and Hogg put Herman on the right track when it came to riding a bucking horse.

Glenbow Archives Photo NA3164-252

There was no success in the bucking contest at Milk River, but later, cowboys were asked if they wanted to ride mount money for $3. You didn't have to stay on any number of seconds — just get on the horse. Even if it bucked you off on the first jump, you got your $3.

While they were bringing his third horse into the chute for Herman, the day's bronc riding winner, Joe Fisher, accompanied by Barney Hogg, stopped and asked Herman if he would like to use their saddle on the next horse.

"Kid," said Fisher, "that short fork saddle would buck off the best rider in the world. How about letting us put a decent outfit on this next horse? Barney and I figure you can make one hell of a good bronc rider."

There were other tips: the stirrup leathers a quarter-inch thick making it hard to spur the horse; spurs too long, so cut them off about half so you can get your foot closer into the horse's flank; cut the chaps down so they fit tight to the leg.

The chute gate swung open and, before Herman knew it, he was out the gate and jolting across the infield. Never had he experienced such a comfortable ride; the motions felt like a rocking chair.

The day ended with Herman buying saddle and braided halter shank for $50 (with the help of a $25 loan from friend Hinman).

He learned an important point that day. Have the right equipment if you want to win money at the rodeo!

With saddle and halter shank in tow, Herman headed to Montana to break horses for a rancher there. He was joined by Gordon DeBray, who had placed third in the roping at Calgary one year and could really handle a lasso. One day, when work was finished, DeBray suggested the two mosey north and have a look at the Calgary Stampede. Along the way, they stopped at Sweetgrass, Montana where Herman won $100 as top bronc rider. The next stop was High River, Alberta, a two-day show just prior to the Calgary rodeo. Some of the top bronc riders of the day were entered at High River and Herman figured his chances of winning were next to nothing. Imagine his surprise when he won first-day money and third-day money in the bareback and one first in saddle bronc day money.

Debray and Herman then headed for Calgary where the "Kid from Cardston" was champion twice over: Canadian Bronc Riding Champion with Saddle and Canadian Bareback Bronc Riding Champion. Added to his winnings at the two smaller shows, Herman now had more than $1,000 and two gold watches. Runner-up in the saddle competition was the immortal Pete Knight of Crossfield, Alberta.

Said Herman: "Winning at Calgary was like a dream. There was more money than I ever hoped to see in my life at one time. One of the greatest thrills of my life was that Saturday night in 1929 at the Stampede grandstand, with fireworks exploding and the crowd cheering the winners of the rodeo. I've had many thrills in my life, but none ever quite like that."

Herman's rodeo career had just begun at the age of twenty-two and the Calgary Stampede would hold many surprises for him in the years ahead.

Herman on the bronc Cheadle at the Calgary Stampede.
Linder Collection

The Peter Welsh Show

George McIntosh "Slim" Leist   "Bud" Shaw   Earl Thode Dick Raeburn   Jack Evans Fred Hewitt Fred Kennedy   Frank

COWBOY CONTESTANTS AT TORONTO STAMPEDE PLACING WRE
Mayor Foster, Bob Carey, Peter Welsh, Mgr. of Toronto Stampede, E M
The Toronto Stampede Sept. 25-Oct. 2, 1926, Was Staged by The Alberta

Participants in the Toronto Stampede, September 25 to October 2, 1926 are seen at the Cenotaph in Toronto. Peter Welsh of the Alberta Stampede Company was in charge of arrangements. From left, are: George McIntosh, "Slim" Leist, "Bud" Shaw, Earl Thode, Dick Raeburn, Jack Evans, Fred Hewitt, Fred Kennedy and Frank Benn. Two others unidentified.
Glenbow Archives Photo NA3164-250

The stampede story would not be complete without mention of Peter Welsh and "Strawberry Red" Woll, who put together a travelling wild west show that played across the nation and into the United States. A fortune would be amassed and lost within the space of four years.

In his book, *Calgary Stampede*, Fred Kennedy tells of Welsh operating the Calgary Horse Sales Repository on Sixth Avenue and Centre Street for a number of years. He had purchased thousands of draught horses for the CPR which would in turn make them available to purchasers of farm lands owned by the railway company.

Somewhere along the line Welsh teamed up with Woll, the cowboy who had made such a hit at the 1919 Calgary Stampede. The two decided to break into the rodeo business and Kennedy tells the rest of the story in Calgary Stampede.

"The requisite of any rodeo operation was a string of top flight bucking horses, so while the 1924 Stampede was being held, they carefully catalogued and graded every bucking horse which came out of the chutes. And they started out to buy them.

"They drove to the Jim MacNab ranch at Fort Macleod, Alberta and when they left the premises two hours later they owned Midnight, the greatest bucking horse of all for a price of five hundred dollars — the highest price paid for a rodeo horse at that time. They then visited the Laycock dairy farm in North Calgary and soon a big pinto named Tumbleweed was added to the string. From there they headed to the Sam Talkington ranch at Bassano where they purchased Bassano, a little fast moving, high kicking, spinning bay horse who was the terror of the irrigation district ninety miles east of Calgary.

"Within a short time they had gathered up about thirty head, and before another year had gone by, Welsh and Woll owned the greatest string of bucking horses the country had ever seen.

"In the summer of 1925, Welsh decided to experiment with three rodeos: Edmonton, Alberta and Vancouver and New Westminster, British Columbia.

"In the contracts, Welsh not only guaranteed that he would produce the world's finest string of bucking horses, but also the cowboy champions to go with them. He had already tagged Pete Knight as a comer, so he got the young Crossfield cowboy into his camp early by buying up Pete's private string of bucking horses. He then signed Pete Vandermeer and some other leading cowboys. So successful were the three shows that Welsh, after dissolving partnership with the temperamental 'Strawberry Red' formed the Alberta Stampede Company of Calgary, with the Hon. R.B. Bennett, later Conservative Prime Minister of Canada, as his chief financial backer.

"Welsh staged successful shows at Winnipeg, Toronto, Montreal, Columbus, Ohio; Buffalo, New York, Detroit, Michigan; Vancouver and New Westminster and did much to groom Pete Knight for his first world's bronc riding title.

"When (Guy) Weadick returned to Calgary in the spring of 1925 and found that Welsh had cornered the bucking horse market, he was annoyed. He had tried unsuccessfully to prevail upon the Exhibition Board to get into the bucking horse business and he felt that Welsh's foray would be an object lesson to the Board. However, in those days, the country was still plentifully supplied with outlaw horses and so the situation was not really serious.

"However, in 1926 and 1927, the Stampede was further embarrassed

Pete Knight helped to make the Alberta Stampede Company a great show.
Jack McCulloch Collection

when a majority of the top riders hit the rodeo trail with Welsh, attracted by the fifteen hundred dollars first money in the saddle bronc riding contest and the promise of a string of six shows in various parts of Canada and the United States. But the supply of cowboys and horses proved unlimited and the Calgary Stampede weathered the storm and successful events again were held."

Welsh's financially strapped rodeo finally bit the dust in Toronto in 1927, when the sheriff moved in and closed the show down.

A Song In Their Hearts

"...Got up quite early. Other members of the family started to arrive about noon. Everybody was jolly. Agnes and I dressed for wedding. Church bells began to ring. The last bell. The Wedding March and sermon. To the photo studio. The big dinner. The great nite."

-Linder diary, Java, South Dakota Sunday, December 25, 1932

Great things came Herman Linder's way in life. The glory of the rodeo arena, the headiness of championships, rubbing shoulders with royalty, world leaders and common folk.

But he believes his shining moment came when he gave his hand in marriage to a shy and beautiful young school teacher, Agnes Zeller, from the American mid-west. The daughter of a European immigrant and successful businessman, she proved to be a steadying influence and loyal helpmate to this young cowboy whose star was just beginning to rise.

They were made for each other. Their union lasted fifty-two years and over that period they followed the rodeo circuit in Canada and the United States, visited Australia twice by passenger liner to take rodeo "Down Under," built a thriving cattle ranch, and established friendships that would span the globe and last a lifetime.

Two children blessed their marriage. George, born June 18, 1942, while Herman was buying bucking horses at the Stettler Rodeo, and Rosemarie, born June 18, 1944, while Herman was at home in Cardston. There would later be seven grandchildren and close relatives on both sides to complete the family circle.

Neighbourliness was also important and they walked through life together for more than half-a-century, with the virtues of modesty and industry ever present.

Following their wedding in the United States, the newlyweds headed home to Cardston over rough roads and deep snows. They arrived there at 5 a.m. New Year's Day, 1933.

For the first six months, the young couple shared a two-room home with the senior Linders. In the evening, a curtain was drawn across the bedroom for the sake of privacy, while older brother Warner slept in the kitchen. Space eased when the school teacher and family who occupied a log cabin on the Linder ranch, moved out when school ended for the summer. In the meantime, the teacher's rent of twenty-five dollars a month was not inconsiderable in those dark Depression days.

Herman's and Agnes' passport photo for 1936.

Linder Collection

Beautiful Agnes smiles for her cameraman husband while taking a stroll in New York. *Linder Collection*

Herman and Agnes moved into the cabin and spent "seven wonderful years" in their log quarters.

In March, 1939, a well was drilled and water struck at forty-nine feet and gravel was hauled for a new Linder house. And on April 17, Warner and Herman started digging the basement for Herman and Agnes' new home. On Nov. 29, 1939, Herman recorded that "Agnes and I spent our very first night in our nice new home and new bed." He concluded the year with this entry Dec. 31: "One of the greatest years of our lives. We had the pleasure of moving into our new home, electric lights and all. We are very happy. Very successful and prosperous year all-around."

Twenty-five-year-old Herman was in his fourth year of prorodeo when he married Agnes.

They met when his future bride came to Cardston in 1931 to visit her sister, Mrs. George (Lena) Wolff, who was married and living in that community.

There was a dance one evening and Herman spotted Agnes, his bride-to-be. She was accompanied by a young farmer from the area, and when the young man took her home and said good night, it had been prearranged that Herman would follow the route and pick up where the young swain had left off.

"Very few people ever knew how our romance got started," chuckled Herman.

Those were light and carefree days for the young couple; just two in love, and going down the road together. Herman riding at the rodeos to make a living and Agnes counting each and every penny so they could carry on; yet save to buy another cow or two for their herd back home. A diary entry made April 25, 1933 showed the two looking at cattle and purchasing five head at sixteen dollars each!

The Linders loved travelling the rodeo circuit, but it was demanding. Agnes admitted that while she was a bit nervous when her husband was going through daring antics with a threshing bull she quite enjoyed the rodeo world.

"I told her when I married her that she'd have to get used to danger," said Herman, "and to her credit, she never complained. Like wives of sporting men all over the world, she became quite involved in my career but she had the good sense not to interfere. That can't be said for all partners of sports people."

There were ranch chores to do in the spring and crops to be put in, and June 20 and 21, 1933 found the two tenting by a creek at Sundre, Alberta.

"... Nice rest in the tent. Entered the show and rode all my stock well. Won first in bareback and bull riding and first in roping. Agnes and I went to the dance in the evening with the Hilmers. Home at midnite."

-Linder diary, June 20, 1933

"... Another good show at Sundre and I won first in bareback, steer and horse riding again, first in decorating and third in roping and second day money in the bronc riding. Rained part of the nite."

-Linder diary, June 21, 1933

Prior to the Calgary Stampede, in the first year of their marriage, Herman competed at Browning, Montana; Carstairs, Carmangay and Midnapore, Alberta — winning or placing throughout.

Herman and Agnes rented a private residence for five dollars a week during the 1933 Calgary Stampede. Meals by Agnes were better and cheaper than the downtown cafes. Top wins in the different events eluded him at Calgary that year. But he wasn't denied his third Canadian All-Around Championship, which would eventually total seven such awards between 1931 and 1938.

Ridin' at the rodeo wasn't without its moments.

The two were at Sidney, Iowa August 18, 1933, and it was the fourth and final day. Herman was down on his luck and trying to borrow some money to leave town — without much success. He drew a rank bull that evening, topped the event and pocketed one hundred and eighty three dollars. "Sure felt tickled," reads Herman's diary for the day.

In the book, *Turn Him Loose*, by Cliff Faulknor, Agnes remembered Sidney and the difficulty finding a place to stay.

There were no motels in those days, just the odd tourist cabin, roughly made affairs, much like a farm granary, with the two-by-four studding bare on the insides. And there were always more customers than there were units to accommodate them.

Herman rides Cheyenne at Sheridan, Wyoming Rodeo with Agnes in the stands.
Doubleday Photo

"Where we stayed in Sidney was just a private home," said Agnes. "Once we arrived to find them busy canning fruit so they could only spare us a small corner of their kitchen to cook our meals. What I remember most about that time is the heat. It was hot weather anyway, and the stoves being on for the canning made it that much worse! But those people were mighty kind to let us stay. They didn't seem to mind the crowding one bit."

As there was only one hotel in Sidney and it was always full, a lot of the cowboys lived in tents. But the Linders seldom did, electing to stay in private homes.

The biggest problem at Sidney was getting meals. Huge crowds used to come to this rodeo because the town was close to several larger centres. At mealtimes, the local restaurants were so crowded there were just no available seats.

Agnes told author Faulknor the couple never used restaurants. "We cooked our own food because we were saving all the money we could to buy cattle for our ranch. In fact, most of our rodeo people stayed out of the restaurants. The tourist cabins or shacks they lived in had stoves and a stack of wood was supplied, so most did their own cooking. The boys who didn't have wives with them, or who weren't married, would eat with the rest. I'd always have two or three boys in to dinner. We were just one big family!"

Another problem on the road was keeping clothes clean. The days of laundromats were yet to come, so every time they stopped, rodeo wives busied themselves washing jeans, shirts, shorts and socks.

Herman at Madison Square Garden, New York in 1933.
Linder Collection

Agnes did a lot of washing for "the boys." She said she had to wash Herman's things, so a few more didn't matter. After the laundry was done in a new town, cupboards in the cabin would be washed out and food put in. A grub box accompanied them on their journeys. Gasoline was around twenty cents a gallon.

Agnes said Cheyenne, Wyoming and Pendleton, Oregon were hard cities for cowboys on the rodeo circuit.

"You had to compete against poor contest judges. You were judged by who knew you. In fact, when Pete Knight first went down there he rode for about two years before anybody even saw him. Then after that, you couldn't beat him. Pete never got any gifts from rodeo — he had to really earn everything he got."

The young wife of the bronc rider said she was glad to travel with Herman, even though it was a long way from home. When the season was over, she was always glad to get back. Then, after a while, they would be missing the travel and those they knew. The Linder friends were travellers, too.

October 29, 1933 found the Linders in New York City visiting the Statue of Liberty, Museum of National History and the Bowery. Herman topped things off by winning a beautiful saddle that year at Madison Square Garden.

On the way back to Niagara Falls and Canada, Herman spotted an airport, and ever the adventurer, took an airplane ride. "Got quite a thrill out of it," he wrote. However, he wasn't too happy with Canadian customs officers who charged him twenty-two dollars for his New York trophy saddle!

"... Agnes felt pretty sick all day. Was in bed 'till noon."
- Linder diary, Dec. 19, 1933

"...Agnes was in bed most of the day. The doctor came and said we could leave for home."
- Linder diary, Dec. 20, 1933

Throughout the diaries that Herman kept for sixty-five years, there were many entries which referred to the health of Agnes, and, in particular, blinding headaches. It was a condition that would recur throughout their married life.

Herman and Johnnie Schneider of Livermore, California, herd cows while in Australia for the Easter Show. Schneider was named World Champion Cowboy by the Rodeo Association of America in 1931. He said, "the best thing about rodeo was that it gave a lot of us a start in life. There weren't that many options back then for a fellow trying to make it." He died in 1982. Linder Collection

Rodeo 'Down Under'

"... A couple on the boat had a fight, she cut the legs off his pants. We played games and visited. The sea is pretty rough today. Played cards."

-Linder diary, Feb. 17, 1936

With this humorous entry, Herman described the first of two trips made to Australia to compete in rodeo at the Royal Agricultural Society Easter Show in Sydney. Attendance would surpass more than one million.

They left Los Angeles February 12, 1936 and would not return to San Francisco until May 16. The big events would last from April 7 to 14 and bronco busting would be called "buckjumping". There was also bull dogging and steer riding.

There were memories to last a lifetime on both trips. There was initiation to the Equator February 19 and shopping in Hawaii February 22 "covered with beautiful flowers." After nearly three thousand miles, they docked at Welllington, New Zealand and then anchored in Sydney harbour March 6.

A week later, Herman and Agnes saw dogs working sheep, wood chopping, camp-drafting and lots of buckjumping. There was also a large kangaroo hunt.

> "...Rainy all day. Had to bulldog again. Sure got terrible dirty. Was a very miserable day."
> -Linder diary, April 12, 1936

Rain would fall at Sydney. It rained so hard April 6 they called off the show. Here's what Herman's diary said about the rest of the rodeo.

> "...It is still rainy. We had the grand finals today. I won the International Buckjumping contest. Also won second in the dogging. Banquet after."
> -Linder diary, April 14, 1936

Much time was spent in the community of Merriwa, watching events like whip cracking and putting on mini-rodeos before Herman and Agnes and other Canadian (including brother Warner) and United States contestants boarded a ship for home April 28. They visited the Fiji Islands, Samoa and Honolulu on their homeward journey. Agnes, dressed up as the mischievous Huckleberry Finn, received the ship's prize for originality at the evening costume ball.

There was another trip to Australia in 1938 at which time Herman headed four Canadian cowboys to compete against teams from the USA, Australia and New Zealand. Accompanying Herman and Agnes were Albertans: Frank McDonald of High River, Jack Wade of Halkirk, and Clark Lund from Raymond. Americans included Milt Moe, Comanche, Oklahoma; Oral Zumwalt, Wolf Creek, Montana; Alvie Gordon, Hollywood, California, and Mel Stonehouse, Cheyenne, Wyoming.

The group sailed from Vancouver, B.C. in good weather on the Canadian-Australasian liner Aorangi February 16 and during the trip, Herman and Agnes would win the best costume title at the ship's ball for coming as Adam and Eve.

Herman seldom, if ever, speaks of getting "messed up" at a rodeo, but he's had his fair share of coming out second best with a horse.

Herman on Matson liner "Mariposa" in harbour at Sydney, Australia.
Russell Roberts photo

Yacht and Sydney Harbour Bridge

Linder Collection

A report from an Australian newspaper dated March 16, 1938 says:

"Herman Linder, 28, leader of the Canadian team of cowboys to appear at the Royal Show, was injured yesterday when a steer unbalanced his horse, which twice rolled on him. He is in Merriwa Hospital.

"Linder is champion buckjumper of Canada and America.

"Yesterday, he and his team-mates conducted an impromptu rodeo at Cullingral, Merriwa. Linder lassoed a steer and when the rope was drawn taut the animal was pulled against his horse, which fell.

"Linder is suffering from concussion and abrasions all over the body. He is expected to fully recover before the Show opens on April 9.

"Linder's wife rushed to the hospital as soon as she heard of her husband's injury."

Herman's description of the same event is recorded in one week of diary entries.

"...I felt terrible sore today. My lips are all swollen up and my eyes swelled shut. Am in lots of pain. Time drags slow."
- Linder diary, March 17

"...I feel sore but am just a little better. I can see out of my right eye. My honey and the boys come to see me."
- Linder diary, March 19

"...Doc said I could go home. My honey came up after lunch and brought me home. She cooked a good American supper for me."
-Linder diary, March 24

Tender nursing by Agnes must have done the trick as Herman won his second International Cup for Buckjumping — both on display at the National Cowboy Hall of Fame in Oklahoma City. Here's the final standings as reported by the Australian press.

Buckjumping: Canada-1, Australia-2, America-3, New Zealand-4. Cup winner: H. Linder, Canada - 352 points.

Bull Dogging: America-1, Australia-2, Canada-3. Best individual score: C. Lund, Canada. Best time: 7-1/2 sec.

Wild Horse Riding: F. McDonald, Canada 11.1.

Canadian Cowboys to Meet 'Aussies'
Canadian "all-round" champion cowboy for six consecutive years, Herman Linder of Cardston, Alberta, is on his way at the head of a contingent of Canadian bronco-busters, to try his luck with Australia's bucking horses at the Royal Agricultural Show at Sydney, April 7-21. Linder is managing the team and is shown here with his wife. The Linders will sail aboard the "Aorangi". With them will be Jack Wade, Halkirk, Alberta; Clark Lund, Milk River, Alberta; and Frank McDonald, Claresholm, Alberta. Four American cowpunchers, Oral Zumalt, Wolfe Point, Montana; Milt Moe, El Reno, Oklahoma; Mel Stonehouse, Chugwater, Wyoming and Alvin Gordon, Helena, Montana, will make the same sailing. W.B. Shelly Photo, Vancouver Sun

Alberta Cowboys to Compete in Australia's Rodeo

Carrying the Maple Leaf emblem in the rodeo to be staged as part of the Royal Easter games in Sydney, Australia, these four hand-picked Canadian riders will ride, rope, bulldog and milk wild cows against four-man teams of American and Australian cowboys. Shown aboard the Canadian-Australian liner, Aorangi, in which they sailed for Australia from Vancouver, the Canadian riders are, left to right, Frank McDonald, High River; Jack Wade, Halkirk; Clark Lund, Raymond and Herman Linder, Cardston, captain.

Calgary Herald Photo

Wild Cow Milking: H. Linder-1, Canada; Miss B. Scott-2, Queensland; O. Zumwalt-3, America.

Herman reported in his diary that he settled up with the Society April 26 and paid income tax on his earnings to the Australian government. (To ensure Canadians and Americans could make the trip to Australia, the Royal Agricultural Society paid each cowboy a certain amount to be a contestant at Sydney.)

The troupe embarked for North America on April 28 and the boys gave Agnes a "beautiful gift" before they reached Los Angeles May 16. The Linders returned with a blue heeler pup called Bobbie, but the dog died shortly after when it was kicked by a horse at the ranch.

Agnes seldom missed the big events in Herman's rodeo life. There was that one time when Herman went to England to perform with Tex Austin's wild west show. She would always smile and say it was a case whether she went with Herman to London or stay home and get a new cook stove. The stove won out.

There were three wonderful journeys, apart from rodeos, that stand out in Herman's memory.

The first trip was to western Europe in 1973 — a trip to a Rotary International convention in Switzerland, seeing the sights of Paris and viewing Maine-Anjou cattle in France, bull fights and centuries-old paintings in Madrid, the ruins of Pompeii from 790 A.D., the Leaning Tower of Pisa, Naples and the Isle of Capri, Rome and St. Peter's Basilica and the Catacombs where early Christians were buried. Then a tour of Austria and the Vienna Woods, a boat trip down the Danube, a stop at a night club and Herman dancing the Blue Danube when "a beautiful lady asked me to dance."

The second trip was to France, August 19 to

When 50,000 People Viewed the Greatest Parade of Livestock Ever Seen in an Australian Show Ring

A section of this parade is illustrated. Here the complete ring is seen as well as the densely-packed stands and ringside lawns, where at least 50,000 people gathered to view the wonderful spectacle on Easter Friday afternoon.

September 3, 1974 meeting many Maine-Anjou cattle breeders and viewing their cattle at different farms.

And finally, with a car and trailer, Herman and Agnes set out for the southern United States on March 14, 1980. It would be the last long jaunt the two would take together and, even then, Herman would write that Agnes "had one of her bad headaches."

There were relatives to visit and old cowboy competitors to talk earlier rodeo days with.

"...We crossed the border at Del Bonita at 11:30 a.m. Arrived home during the noon hour. Granddaughter Nancy came running out to meet us. We stopped at George's and visited for an hour. We are so thankful the Dear Lord brought us home, it was a wonderful trip we had."

- Linder diary, May 10, 1980

Throughout the years of his diaries, Herman faithfully recorded the involvement of Agnes and himself in community and church life. There was hardly a Sunday, when at home, they were not in the pews of their small Lutheran Church in Cardston. Today's church organ is a gift of the Linder family in memory of Agnes, wife and mother. And there was the special day marking fifty years of wedded life when relatives and friends joined the Linders to celebrate their anniversary.

The Linder marriage was remarkable for two people getting along for more than five decades. There is one entry only of Herman expressing regret at saying something out of line. He told of a trip to Lethbridge, "drinking a little too much Scotch and making an ass of myself driving home."

"... I feel bad about my actions last night. Mother feels blue too. I told Mother I was sorry about last night and I really meant it. I hope it never happens again."

-Linder diary January 7, 1975

She Keeps Smiling For The Cowboy She Loves

"... Big Boy sure got the best of me November 11. Several days in hospital getting healed."

- Linder diary, November 20, 1935

Wife of Bronc Rider Injured At Rodeo Displays Magnificent Courage

(The Boston Evening American, November, 1933)

BY DOROTHY WAYMAN

It's fine to see the courage some folks have ... and the time to see it is in an emergency like yesterday afternoon when Herman Linder, ranchman from Alberta and bronc rider at the rodeo, was thrown and trampled by Big Boy, whom other cowboys call the most vicious bronco of them all.

Herman's wife, Agnes, was not in the arena when it happened. She was packing up at their apartment so they could leave for home the next day.

First thing the other cowboys thought of, even as they were lifting Herman's unconscious, broken body from the ground and carrying it off in a stretcher, was his wife. They are big and brawny and tough as steel, those bronc-busting cowboys, but they're shy where women come in. Owen Wister knew that as well and described it in *The Virginian.*

Well the cowboys came running to ask me if I would stand by Herman's wife. So I rode in the ambulance and I waited at the hospital with her — and I saw two people with magnificent courage and affection for each other.

She was white as skim milk and shaking like a leaf, but she held her chin up and kept back her tears.

"I've got to smile for Herman or he'll think he's hurt real bad," she said. "Oh, dear God, if only his back isn't broken. If it's just some bones, they'll get better soon. Herman heals quick. He was in the hospital before and he healed just wonderfully.

"I hope he isn't like Curley. He's the blonde cowboy that brought you over to me. Curley was thrown two years ago and he broke his neck. He had to lie flat in a cast for nine months.

"I didn't know Herman was a bronc-rider when I fell in love with him. I guess I couldn't have stood it if I knew it then. I was teaching school in South Dakota in those years and Herman was introduced to me at a Thanksgiving dance in Alberta where I was visiting. We were engaged by Christmas and right soon after we got married.

"You know, we have a ranch out in Cardston, Alberta. But it's been hard times for cattlemen. We were hard up, too. Then there was a rodeo and Herman said he'd be busy that day but why didn't I go with some of the girls.

"And the first thing I knew he came riding out on top of a bucking bronc. Well, Herman's awfully good at it, and it's our living now, what he makes on prize money. But I'll be so glad when cattle

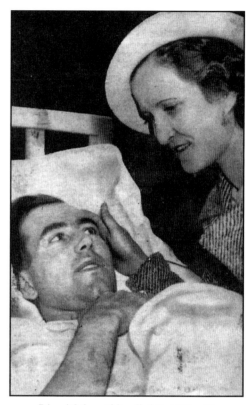

It's with heartfelt relief that Mrs. Herman Linder, visiting her injured rodeo-rider husband at the Massachusetts General hospital, finds that his temperature is coming down and his face is no longer burning with the fever which was the aftermath of his nearly fatal accident at the Boston Garden. She plans to take him to the home of her parents at Eureka, South Dakota, as soon as he is able to travel. Linder's own home is in Cardston, Alberta, Canada.

Boston Evening American Photo 1935

48

come back and we can just settle down on the ranch.

"I never see him getting ready to ride, that I don't whisper a little prayer. I hope my prayer was heard today and Herman will be all right."

They won't know 'til tomorrow, maybe longer, how badly Herman is hurt. X-rays have to be taken at the Baker Memorial Hospital, where he is a patient and surgeons have to poke and probe to find out just how much damage those stamping hooves of Big Boy did.

Meanwhile his wife, Agnes Linder, is all alone in a strange city, two thousand miles from her relatives and friends, pacing a hotel room all night wondering, worrying, praying.

The cowboys all tried to help every way they could. They stood around Herman's unconscious body in the arena, blocking off the wild attack of the vicious bronc, fanning Herman ineffectually with their ten-gallon hats. It was all they could think of to do and they had to do something.

There was big Dick Shelton and John Bowman, the pick-up men who would have given an arm if they could have reached Herman in time to snatch him from those stamping hooves. There was Jimmy Nesbitt and Jasbo Fulkerson, the clowns, smearing the paint on their faces with fingers that brushed something from smarting eyes. Shorty Hill picked up Herman's chaps and hat as they lifted him onto the stretcher for the ambulance ride. John Jordan, the good-looking announcer at the amplifier, had a frog in his throat when he tried to "go on with the show."

All the boys like Herman and they know Agnes has not been strong. It broke them all up to have this happen on the last day of the rodeo, with their bags packed to start home tomorrow.

So there were Agnes and I sitting in a hospital waiting room while upstairs doctors and nurses did things for Herman.

Then the nurse came to say Agnes could go upstairs. The nurse took one look at the girl's drawn, white face and whispered to me, "You'd better go with her in case she keels over."

She didn't keel over. She went in with a smile like it was Christmas Day and she leaned over and kissed him, saying: "You'll be better in the morning. I'll be back in the morning after you have a good sleep."

The nurse had a printed form ready.

"This is a necessary formality," she explained. "The patient must sign a statement as to whether he brought any valuables to the hospital with him."

That was funny. Because before they put Herman in the ambulance, they had stripped his clothes off for an emergency examination and then wrapped him in a blanket while Shorty Hill picked up his clothing.

Herman grinned. In all his pain and weakness, he grinned. And he said to the nurse: "I don't need to sign that. My 'valuables' is going to walk out of the hospital in a moment on her own two feet."

Herman and Agnes ... in Herman's rodeo managing years.
Glenbow Archives NA3253-3

Fan Mail For A Cowboy

When Herman Linder was injured by a bronc at Boston Garden in November, 1935, he was deluged with letters of encouragement and support by the people of Boston.

Some would send greetings, some a small sum of money, and some offered to put Herman and Agnes up in their home until Herman was able to travel back to Canada.

Here are two letters among the many that Agnes saved:

November 14, 1935

Dear Mr. Linder:

I read in the paper that you were lonely. Well I've been thinking of you every day wondering how you were. I am certainly glad to hear you are getting better as I saw you ride and I think you are a good rider.

I am eight years old next month and I'm eating spinach and cereal so I will grow up quick and go to work and buy a horse. I want to ride like you. I bet you are waiting for some of those lush pancakes. I am going to ask my mother if she knows how to make them and make me some.

I hope a lot of other boys and girls will write to you to cheer you and Mrs. Linder. Don't be lonely as I will be thinking of you when I'm in school 'cause I want to see you next year again.

Yours truly,

Donald Kimball,
37 Mattapan Street,
Mattapan, Mass.

November 13, 1935

Dear Mrs. Linder:

I read in last evening's *Evening American* the account of your tragedy and remarkable courage as written by reporter Dorothy Wayman.

I do hope by now that you have heard good news and that it will be but a short time before all is well and you are again on your way.

I have long been an admirer of cowboys and rodeo and in fact most anything that symbolized the great outdoors.

I am enclosing a tiny sum of money which I wish you would accept as a token of my appreciation of bravery. I am a terrible coward and so shrink from pain.

If I can do anything to lighten your stay in Boston won't you drop me a line or phone me at Jamaica 3099-77. I keep house for my dad and brother and usually have a fair amount of spare time. When my mother was alive I worked as a stenographer.

Wishing you and your husband the best of luck for a speedy recovery and hoping to hear from you if you feel lost or lonely.

Cordially yours,
Emma M. Oetinger
200 South Huntington Avenue
Jamaica Plain, Boston, Mass.

Agnes' Little Black Book

The key to a financially successful rodeo career was a little black book.

That's how Agnes Linder recalled the family's "high financing" back in the Depression Years.

Speaking to reporter Garry Allison of *The Lethbridge Herald*, Agnes said that during Herman's rodeo life, she carried a little black book and kept track of "absolutely everything," from five-cent chocolate bars to hotel or rooming expenses.

She accompanied her husband to all the rodeos he competed in during the 1930s, from Australia's "down under" to New York's Madison Square Garden; Boston, Massachusetts and Montreal, Quebec in the east, to places like Lewiston, Idaho, Cheyenne, Wyoming and Calgary, Alberta. The only trip she didn't make was to England.

"Our rodeo life was a little like a honeymoon," she says. "We went to all the rodeos together, it wasn't that hard — and I kept my black book — that's an easy way to save money."

The Linders celebrated their fifty-second wedding anniversary in 1984, at which time Agnes remembered her first drive to the Linder ranch on a bitter, cold New Year's Eve in 1932 only a few days after they were married. The old Chrysler, which they were driving, got stuck in the snow and a neighbour had to harness his team and pull the newlyweds home.

"Times were hard in those early days. We even had the telephone taken out because we couldn't afford the $1.50," Agnes recalled. "We had no radio, just a carry-all phonograph. Dad Linder was a good card player and we played bridge every night, with the school teacher joining us — the couple that sat out pulled wool for carding."

Agnes said she was "too green" to worry about Herman injuring himself in a rodeo arena in those early days, but she told reporter Allison she'd do it all over again, mainly because of the friendships they built.

"I won't lie. I was Herman's worst critic and I still am," she said in her last interview. "Rodeo life then was what you wanted to make it — there were both sides of life."

FRIENDSHIP

*Life is sweet because
of the friends we have made
And the things which in common we share
We want to live on,
not because of ourselves
But because of the people who care.
It's in giving and doing,
for somebody else
On all that life's splendor depends
And the joys of this life,
when you've summed it all up
Are found in the making of friends.*

- A plaque in the Linder kitchen

A Time To Say Goodbye

"...We took mother to the airport by ambulance and Rosemarie and I accompanied her on the jet to London, Ontario. Ken Muir and Mary Daw were with us."

Linder diary November 27, 1984

Agnes' health had not been the best through 1984 and, eventually, she was hospitalized in both Cardston and Calgary's Foothills Hospital before a decision was made to send her to a neurosurgeon in London, Ontario for the removal of a brain tumour.

"...They brought mother from the operating room at 5 p.m. The doctors came and told us the operation was successful, but they said she would have bad headaches."

-Linder diary November 30, 1984

Nearly five months passed, and Agnes was once again admitted into the Foothills Hospital in Calgary April 14, 1985 for another operation. A minor stroke followed the surgery leaving Agnes unable to move her left hand or left leg.

"...Dr. Myles told me they are not pleased with Mother and will give her a cat scan. He later took us into the little room and told us Mother would soon be leaving us. Felt very sad. We called home and talked to Kia. I sat up with Mother all night."

- Linder diary, April 24, 1985

Arrangements were made to transfer Agnes to the Cardston Hospital to be closer to her family. She arrived late in the evening of April 26. It was the closest she would get to her beloved ranch home on the rolling plains of southern Alberta.

The Linder family (Herman, Agnes, George and Rosemarie) in earlier days.
Linder Collection

"... (Daughter-in-law) Kia (a Registered Nurse) phoned to say Mother was passing away. When I got to the hospital she had just left to go to our Dear Lord in Heaven."

-Linder diary April 27, 1985

And so she was gone. The sweetheart of his youth, loyal companion of his rodeo days, faithful wife and mother. The days of wine and roses had come to an end. Herman's diary summed it up:

"...Went to son George's for New Year's Eve. The girls had hats for us all. We joined hands and sang Auld Lang Syne. Of course, this past year was very sad for me. No one really knows how sad things can be until you have the experience of losing your lifemate. I am lucky to have three wonderful granddaughters so close. They are a great comfort to me."

-Linder diary, December 31, 1985

Agnes and granddaughter.
Linder Collection

Postscript: The funeral for Agnes Linder was held in Cardston on April 30, 1985. She died at the age of seventy-six after fifty-two years of marriage. Her great loves were her home and family, the Lutheran Church to which she belonged and her flower garden. The Linders had two children: George (and Kia) who had taken on the ranching duties at Linder and Son Ranch; and daughter, Rosemarie (married to Tommy Bews of Longview, Alberta, who also had an outstanding rodeo career).

George and wife Kia and three children resided on the ranch. On Sunday, January 5, 1986, the family found George dead by his truck. He had been feeding cattle in the field. He was forty-four years of age. Death was due to heart failure. His funeral was held at Cardston January 8, 1986.

No Sad Tears For Me, Please ...

"... Ran across something Mother wrote. It was so nice. No Tears, Please. It really broke me up and I just couldn't help but shed tears. Granddaughter Nancy came over for awhile this eve and we shed tears together. I miss Mother so much. So all alone in this house, and today, after I read what she wrote, was really sad for me."

-Linder diary, November 11, 1985

Thanksgiving, Christmas, Easter, birthdays and anniversaries were always special in the Linder household, and when Agnes Linder died in 1985 it was up to Herman to carry on the tradition of sending Christmas cards to friends and relatives — some close by and some at distant points in the world.

Here's the Christmas letter he sent out in the year of Agnes' passing:

Christmas, 1985

On November 11, I found this letter written by my dear wife, Agnes. I am sure she knew, eventually I would find it. As things unfolded she knew for several months that our Dear Lord was going to call her home. She wrote with a pen and there were a few places that were almost unreadable from her fallen tear drops.

This letter will take the place of her Christmas letter that so many of you enjoyed reading. Many of your sympathy cards indicated you will miss the Christmas letter this year, so I want to share her letter with you.

Dear Loved Ones:

I hope by now the initial shock of my departure has begun to wear away, and that the kind carpet of pleasant memories has started to unroll. I only ask one thing: No sad tears for me, please.

Every wonderful, delightful thrill, experience and emotion life has to offer has been mine. So, no tears for me, please. Rather, recall me with a fond smile as the mother and friend who shared your laughter, tears and dreams through the years.

Save your sadness and sorrow for those who go before their time, for those who leave before they taste all the fine fruits of the world. No sad tears for me, please.

I lived a good span of years and I enjoyed them all. I've laughed a lot, cried a little. I've seen a thousand sunsets and fresh dawns, walked in the rain and saw the wheat fields wave.

I loved a man, and was loved in return, and walked with my grandchildren. No sad tears for me, please.

Many victories were mine, and they gave life zest. I've had defeats and they made me strong. Life was good. I saw robins and meadowlarks in the spring, watched a shooting star, watched buttercups grow, enjoyed the snow in the winter, walked under a harvest moon and stood on top of a hill and saw the flickering lights of town. No sad tears, please.

Think of the happy times: the Christmas mornings, the graduations, the Thanksgiving dinners and fun along the riverbank; but, most of all, remember the times we were all together as a family, No sad tears, please.

For no one dies as long as there is someone left who kindly remembers them. So, on Christmas Eve, if there is a small star in the sky, look at it with love and let it come into your heart and remember me. It is said God heals all wounds and replaces them with pleasant memories we shared. No sad tears, please. Bye.

I am getting along as well as can be expected. As this year comes to an end I wish you all a very Merry Christmas and a Happy New Year.

With love,

Herman

Brother Warner A Champion In His Own Right

"...Brother Warner has gone over the Great Divide. But the Dear Lord is good and my brother didn't have to suffer long. I am so sad."

—*Linder diary, October 27, 1983*

There was no doubt in Herman Linder's mind that if brother Warner had decided to follow the rodeo trail, he would have been a star in both roughstock and timed events.

Instead, he elected to spend most of his time on the ranch, helping with crops and cattle operations.

Warner was born March 21, 1906 in Wisconsin and was twelve years old when the family started their ranch in the Canadian west in 1918.

Herman and Warner were great friends and rode horseback to the one-room Dolan School. And, in grade eight exams of the early 1920s, Warner would eclipse all students of the south, from town, city or village and win the Governor-General's Medal for Excellence for the year. "He was smart, no doubt about it," says Herman.

The two boys made their own fun on the ranch and, when not helping their dad with the chores, they would ride wild steers and stray range horses (either bareback with surcingle or with saddle).

Writing in *West Magazine*, Calgary Stampede founder, Guy Weadick, a good friend of the Linders, had this to say about their riding ability:

"Warner seemed to be the hard-luck rider of the two. His mounts seemed to fall with him, run into things, or into or over fences that would result in severely bruised or broken bones. They were always pals, and Herman claims that, as a rider, his brother was better than he was. His own success is due, more than anything else, to Warner's help and advice."

Despite his commitment to the ranch, Warner found time to enter rodeos at Cardston, Shelby, Montana, Calgary, Fort Macleod and other centres close to home.

And, like brother Herman, he also found the winner's circle. He was champion steer decorator at the Calgary Stampede in 1935, 1936 and

Warner Linder was a champion in his own right.

Linder Collection

1938 and won the calf roping title in 1936. Here's how the Calgary press reported his efforts in the latter year:

"Warner Linder of Cardston emerged as North American champion steer decorator and Canadian calf roping champion. He performed the most spectacular feat of this year's show by making a flying tackle with his crippled back in a T-splint, to set a world's record for consecutive wild steer decorating and practically equalled the feat Saturday by roping and tying a calf in fast time to capture the Canadian championship in this event. With collarbone broken and ligaments torn, his back was still in a brace."

The Cardston weekly newspaper reported in its June 23, 1936 issue: "Warner Linder, Cardston's own cowboy, clipped more than a second from the world's steer decorating record when he hung the ribbon on the horn in three seconds flat. He also took first in calf roping here at Cardston."

Warner was named North American champion steer decorator for 1938 by the Rodeo Association of America at its annual convention January, 1939 at the Murray Hotel in Livingston, Montana.

Although the Linder brothers were close, there was an edginess to their relationship. Herman noted that his brother would disappear two or three days at a time, leaving others to do the ranch work.

In addition, Herman could not interest Warner in expanding their ranching operations. Said Herman: "We had an opportunity to buy three sections of productive land for $50,000. A great place for Warner and his wife to live and raise cattle. But they didn't like the buildings on the land and the purchase was turned down. I wouldn't speculate on what that land is worth today."

There were strong words between the brothers in the spring of 1958 (again for Warner's prolonged absences from the ranch). The brothers finally agreed to separate when a threshing crew was held up an entire morning when Warner simply failed to appear. Warner moved off the home quarter August 14, after forty years of residence.

Warner and wife Rozella eventually purchased a residence in town. (Rozella is ninety-two years old and lives in an extended care home in Cardston.) The two brothers were always cordial in their dealings, constantly visited back and forth and (with their wives) played bridge, whist and cribbage. And they jointly planned their eighty-one-year-old mother's (Marie) funeral in 1960, for whom they had bought a house in town some years before.

Warner's death came unexpectedly.

He was eating chicken at home on October 23, 1983 when he suddenly choked and slumped unconscious to the floor. His wife called a friend, a registered nurse, who summoned an ambulance and he was taken to a Calgary hospital. The lungs were badly congested and Warner could not breathe on his own. Placed on life support, he died four days later on October 27 at age seventy-seven.

He is buried beside his mother and father in the Cardston cemetery.

Brothers Warner and Herman Linder are seen at the "Little Royal", Fort Macleod Auction Market. Joining them are Herman's son, George, and granddaughters Nancy and Sarah.   *Alberta Beef photo*

World Series Rodeo

MADISON SQUARE GARDEN —— NEW YORK CITY

OCTOBER 1931.

Winning Big At Madison Square Garden

It was the greatest of times in the lives of Herman and Agnes Linder when he won the bareback title and came in second in saddle bronc riding and was named All-Around Cowboy at the 1933 Madison Square Garden, New York City World Series rodeo. Madison Square Garden president Col. J.R. Kilpatrick is seen far left and beside him is rodeo producer Col. W.T. Johnson, who quit producing rodeo following the Boston strike of 1936. Herman is seen with other rodeo champions of that year and holding tightly to the beautiful saddle he won at New York. Linder collection.

By every radio and newspaper account in October, 1933, Herman had found the pot of gold at the end of the rainbow at the Eighth Annual World Series of Rodeo in Madison Square Garden, New York, New York.

"With six others who won less important championships, Linder will share $42,000 in prize money," gladly trumpeted the Canadian news media.

But it wasn't as good as it sounded. It's true Herman won more money than any other contestant in the fall spectacular (about $1,800 in different events), but pay-outs for daily winnings for cowboys and cowgirls had seriously eroded the $42,000.

Herman was presented with a beautiful hand-tooled trophy saddle by Colonel John R. Kilpatrick, Garden president, at the conclusion of the show and declared bareback and All-Around Champion. This being the first saddle he had ever won in competition, he placed it by his bedside and kept wakening during the night to reach out and touch the saddle to make sure it was still there.

Noted a cowboy competitor in the now defunct *Hoofs and Horns* magazine: "Everyone likes Linder. He's as popular in New York as in Calgary. He's a first-class man in the arena and he's clean as a whistle. He's a great rider and he's just getting started."

Herman and Agnes whistled a merry tune as they headed back to Niagara Falls, Ontario and Herman would splurge by taking a ride in an airplane when they passed a small airport.

Two events served to bring him rudely down to earth.

Crossing the border into Canada, customs officials admired the saddle and then charged Herman $18 duty. His protests regarding a rodeo gift rang on deaf ears.

Some time later, the income tax fellows in Ottawa were looking for a big bite of the "lion's share" of $42,000. Herman had no trouble explaining that the pot of gold at the end of the rainbow was just that. And still there!

COL. W.T. JOHNSON AND HIS WORLD'S

AMPIONSHIP RODEO CONTESTANTS.

Col. W.T. Johnson and his world's championship rodeo contestants, New York City, October 7, 1936

Linder Collection

59

Burel Mulkey, Earl Thode and Johnny Jordan were great bronc riders and many-times champions.
Linder Collection

Bucking Broncs Of Yesteryear

"... Here in Chicago, cloudy and raining. I rode all my stock OK. But didn't place in any of it. No luck in wild horse race. Harry Knight bucked off and is hurt very bad. Had to go on parade in eve."

—Linder diary, August 27, 1933

Things would get better for Herman as the rodeo progressed in Chicago and a horse named *Ham What Am* played a critical role in his career.

He drew the horse at the World's Fair in Chicago in 1933, before he'd made a name for himself as one of the all-time great rodeo cowboys and long before people thought of him as "Canada's Mister Rodeo".

He recalls he was getting aboard *Ham What Am*, a bay horse weighing about thirteen hundred pounds and about as tough as they came. He wasn't too showy but brought down some of the best riders during his rodeo life.

"Earl Thode of Belvidere, South Dakota, a world champion bronc

rider, walked by and suggested I shorten my rein a bit. If he hadn't offered those words of advice that bronc would have bucked me off for sure. I'd have gone right over his head," said Herman. Instead, he won top day money.

That was the turning point in Linder's life. He says riding *Ham What Am* gave him courage and recognition. From then on he started winning money at nearly all the rodeos in one event or another.

Ham What Am was not the best bronc Linder ever rode, though. That honour goes to *Pardner*.

The old black horse, which Linder and brother Warner used to ride as

Herman on Anchor Boy

Herman on Payday at Colorado Springs Rodeo.

Doubleday Photo

The late Turk Greenough bronc riding at the rodeo in Sidney, Iowa.
Linder Collection.

The "Canada Kid" steer riding at the Calgary Stampede.

Famous bronc rider Turk Greenough of Red Lodge, Montana, was in the U.S. army with his new bride, Sally Rand, when he sent this postcard to Herman and Agnes Linder from Cheyenne, Wyoming, July 27, 1942. Sally was noted for her fan dancing and was a dancer and actress for forty-five years. She appeared in several movies including "Getting Gertie's Garter." Sally was born in 1904 and died in 1979.
Doubleday photo.

kids at the Linder ranch, went on to become a great saddle bronc. He says had *Pardner* started bucking earlier in his life, he would have earned a reputation as large as that of *Midnight* or *Five Minutes to Midnight,* two of the greatest bucking horses in history.

Pardner, renamed *School Boy Rowe* in New York after the baseball pitcher, was fourteen hundred pounds and broken to ride. But put him into a chute and he was ready for action. Warner once rode the horse into Cardston to perform for rodeo producer Ray Knight. *Pardner* impressed Knight by bucking off three riders.

"I drew him (*Pardner*) in Boston in 1938 and this time I got by him to win day money. I had ridden him only once before at the ranch."

Pardner bucked in Indianapolis, New York and Boston and was only ridden four times in 1935 when he was at least fifteen years old. By 1939, *Pardner* was nineteen and still one of the best ten horses in rodeo. To Herman's way of thinking, *Pardner* was one of the great bucking horses of all time.

As the old rodeo rhyme goes: "There never was a horse that can't be rode, or ever a cowboy that can't be thrown."

Herman says *Easy Money* was no slouch either. "You didn't want to make any mistake or he would flatten you out. He was a beautiful sorrel and weighed at least sixteen hundred pounds."

In the annals of rodeo, it is agreed that *Midnight* and *Five Minutes To Midnight* were the best of the roughstock bunch.

Midnight, owned by Jim McNab of Fort Macleod, Alberta, got started in rodeo by tossing an Indian cowboy who had mounted him to ride to the chuck wagon for grub during a round-up on the nearby Blood Reserve in Southern Alberta.

Midnight made his first appearance at the Calgary Stampede in 1924. After tossing every cowboy who was unlucky enough to draw him, the horse's fame soon spread. He was finally bought by Woll and Welsh of the Alberta Stampede Company Ltd. for $500.

When Alberta Stampede went broke, *Midnight* and *Five Minutes to Midnight*, both Alberta horses, were purchased by American Jim Eskew who wanted them for his wild west outfit. They proved too tough, so he brought them to Fort Worth, Texas and sold them to Ed McCarty and Verne Elliott.

The great horse, Midnight, and owner Jim McNab of Fort Macleod, Alberta.

Linder Collection

The two horses made their first appearance in the Big Time at Fort Worth, Texas in 1929.

Lee Farris, better known as "Canada Kid" drew *Five Minutes To Midnight* in the first go-round. The horse quickly tossed him into space. Then Earl Thode drew *Midnight*. He lasted until the fourth jump.

Don Nesbitt, writing in *Persimmon Hill*, said *Midnight* was much gentler to handle than *Five*. He spent most of his days in a box stall with the special attention due him while *Five* just plain did not like or trust humans. He was about twenty years old at the time.

"The size, action, style and temperament of the two were completely opposite but they both brought the same end results to the cowboy with alarming regularity. They just plain didn't get rode!"

Midnight stood about fifteen-and-a-half hands, was active as a cat and weighed in at twelve hundred pounds while *Five* was just eight hundred and ninety-five pounds, and fourteen-and-a-half hands of black dynamite.

"Where *Midnight* bucked the boys off with sheer strength, *Five* was a thinking critter and when he wasn't getting his job done one way, he'd change his style in midstream and so compensated for his lack of size with determination and smarts," wrote Nesbitt who managed to stay aboard *Five Minutes to Midnight* in 1932 at Deadwood, South Dakota, the same year he won the All Around World's championship. He drew *Midnight* just once and never finished his ride.

Midnight, world famous bucking horse doing his stuff.

Outwest Photo Service

Leaving Calgary for London, England to take part in a Wild West rodeo in 1934 are these top rodeo contestants from the Alberta plains: Herman Linder, Harry Knight, Pat Burton, Jackie Cooper, Jackie Streeter, Norman Edge and an unidentified cowboy. In the rear is Clark Lund.   *Linder Collection*

Midnight went to England in 1934 for a thirty-three day contest engineered by rodeo promoter Tex Austin and bucked everybody except Alvie Gordon who won the bronc riding in London.

Two cowboys making qualified rides on *Five* were Pete Knight and Doff Aber. Pete rode him twice in 1934 at Portland, Oregon and around 1936 in Fort Worth. Doff got the job done in Los Angeles in 1935.

"Those two horses were tops and commanded the respect of every cowboy in the business. They had fans all over the country who would fill the stands when it was reported that one of the two stars would be competing," wrote Nesbitt.

The men bucked off the pair of horses was a "Who's Who of Rodeo" including: Turk Greenough, Johnny Jordan, Nick Knight, Fritz Truan, Bill Linderman, Harry Knight, Cecil Henley, Pete Knight, Burel Mulkey, Leo Murray, Hub Whiteman, Ward Watkins, Breezy Cox, Earle Thode and Freckles Brown.

As it turned out, Herman Linder drew neither horse in his long rodeo career. But he recalls other champion broncs including: *Hell's Angel, Stamp, Black Diamond, Patches, War Paint, Bear Tooth, Harry Tracey, Brown Jug, Dizzy Dean* and *Red Gold.*

"Leo Cramer always had a lot of real tough horses in his string. A horse I bought for Leo at Kalispell, which he named *Lee Rider*, turned out to be a real tough horse during the 'Forties. He was a grey gelding , probably weighing around thirteen hundred pounds. Not too many rode him either," says Herman.

He said the horse that killed Pete Knight was a tough one. His name was *Duster*, and he was coal black. Harry Rowell of Hayward, California owned him.

Horses owned by E.C. Colburn and the World Championship Rodeo Company, the Doc Sorenson string, the Oral Zumwalt string, the Christenson Bros. string and Harry Knight's string, all contributed immeasurably to the rodeo circuit.

But to hear Knight tell it to Fred Kennedy: *"Five Minutes to Midnight* would actually rate a few notches above the redoubtable *Midnight* because of his speed, sunfishing, and twisting ability and his spectacular all around performance. But from a

London, England was the place and Buckingham Palace on the visitor's list as Herman (right) and Mel Bascom pose with a guard. The two were taking part in a rodeo at White City, London in 1934.

Linder Collection

Herman on Goofus

bronc rider's point of view, it was just possible that *Midnight* would still get the nod as the world's all time great bucking horse because of his tremendous power and his unequalled buck-off record."

Midnight's bucking career progressed until he was retired in 1933 at the end of Cheyenne's Frontier Days in Wyoming.

After many appearances at various rodeos for the next three years, he died at Denver in 1936. A full funeral was held for the outlaw horse and his remains were buried under the shade trees at Verne Elliott's Platteville, Colorado, ranch where a headstone was erected. The remains were later exhumed and placed in a special plot at the National Cowboy Hall of Fame in Oklahoma City. *Five* also died at Elliott's and was buried beside *Midnight*.

Medicine Hat Horse A Tough One

Foaled on the H2 Ranch south of Medicine Hat, Alberta, in 1906, the big sorrel gelding *No Name*, was broke and used to haul gravel as a five-year-old. In 1911 he bucked at a small rodeo near Calgary and the following year was one of the top horses at the inaugural 1912 Calgary Stampede where he bucked off four riders.

Known as *Reservation*, he was the feature horse of the famed Day and Knight string of bucking stock for several years. In 1916 his name was changed to *I Don't Know*. (Stock contractors would often change the name of a bucking horse to confuse contestants. Cowboys would learn all they could about the way a horse bucked to get an edge on their mount. However, if they didn't recognize the name they could hardly know the horse before the chute gate opened. i.e. the bronc that killed Pete Knight was not only known as *Duster*, but also as *Slowdown*, hence, some confusion over the name of the horse Pete rode that day.)

At the 1919 Calgary Stampede, scouts for the Pendleton Round Up bought the horse then known as *Fox* for $1,500 from Walt McHugh. The Pendleton Association renamed him *No Name* and featured him for the next seven years. In 1926 they retired him with ceremony and the next year he was buried along the Columbia River in a country known as Horse Heaven.

He was named to the Honour Roll of Great Bucking Horses at the National Cowboy Hall of Fame in Oklahoma City in 1977.

Herman rides Hot Tamale.

The Cowboy Travels To Merrie England

It was billed as the World's Championship Rodeo at White City, London, England from June 9 to July 6, 1934 presented by the National Sporting Club Ltd. and producer Tex Austin of the United States. Financially, it was a flop, but it gave Londoners an opportunity to view a Wild West show over three and a half weeks.

Herman joined a band of Alberta cowboys in Calgary May 4 and travelled by train to Montreal where they were joined by a group of Americans, leaving by ship on May 16.

By looking after the stock on their way across the ocean, their passage was paid. Money would come later, depending on their prowess in the rodeo arena.

Herman shared a room with Norman Edge of Cochrane, Alberta while in London and the two did lots of sightseeing including the races at Epsom Downs, Windsor Castle, Ascot Downs and Hampton Court. He also had his picture taken with a sentry at Buckingham Castle.

Back at the rodeo, Herman was winning money in the saddle bronc, bareback, wild horse race and steer riding.

But this time, "Lucky" Linder's luck didn't last. While stepping off a horse, he turned his ankle which put him out of the finals.

He purchased a ticket from his winnings aboard the Empress of Britain and sailed home June 23 with Pat Burton of Claresholm, Alberta. They arrived in Quebec June 28 and Lethbridge, Alberta July 2nd where he was met by wife Agnes. Nothing to do but head a few miles down the road to Raymond, Alberta where Herman won both the riding and roping honours. A day later he was entered at Carmangay, Alberta where he won first in the saddle bronc and roping and second in the bareback event.

And what about things back in White City? Although the stadium had seating for one hundred thousand, there was a wilderness of empty seats. But the show did go on.

Viscount Castlerose, reporting for a London newspaper had this comment: "If you get a man as hard as nails, as brave as a lion, as active as a cat, as lithe as a serpent, then you have a cowboy."

As for the children in attendance? They liked all the action but expressed their disappointment their cowboy heroes wore no guns.

Fairs Go Back A Long Way

Fairs go back to Biblical times, being mentioned in the book of Ezekiel. The Greeks and Romans held fairs and in the time of Alfred The Great fairs were known in England. The Lee Horse Fair in Yorkshire has been held for more than seven hundred years!

The first International Fair was held in London, England in 1851, while the first fair in Toronto was held in 1846, now the Canadian National Exhibition.

Alberta's first fair was in Calgary, October 9, 1886 and Lethbridge hosted its first fair in 1896. Sixteen years later, Lethbridge hosted the World Dryland Wheat Congress, patronized by fifteen countries and proving to be the largest show of its kind at that time.

The Lethbridge and District Exhibition was the first fair in Western Canada to go to a fall livestock show — The Rocky Mountain Livestock Show.

Herman Linder produced summer rodeos at Lethbridge for several years and, in 1967, he was made a member of the Exhibition's Hall of Fame.

HG Photo

they were in crashed into a snowy mountain top in the remote Uinta Mountains near Coalville, Utah. According to son Peter, his dad's career started at the age of sixteen and he later won all of the major rodeos, including Calgary in 1940 (North American saddle), Cheyenne, Wyoming in 1938, Fort Worth, Texas; Pendleton, Oregon and many more. A major story by Bob Wiseman featured Nick Knight and the fifteen-hand bay gelding Badger Mountain in the Summer, 1996 issue of The Ketchpen, published by the Rodeo Hall of Fame, Oklahoma City, Oklahoma. Knight was the only one to ride the great saddle bronc Badger Mountain, not once, but three times. A top rodeo writer once wrote: "The horse bolted lightning fast from the irritating confines of a narrow chute, became a scheming demon of bucking destruction, eleven hundred pounds of conniving, thinking horseflesh, working in a fashion so fast and methodically furious that no mortal man, not even the best, could stay topside for ten seconds." All, except Nick Knight, that is. In 1954, when members of the Rodeo Cowboys Association were polled by the Levi Strauss Company, Badger Mountain was named one of the three greatest bucking horses of all time.

Herman is seen with Nevada lawyer Peter L. Knight during the annual meeting of the Rodeo Historical Society in Las Vegas in December, 1995. Peter is the son of the late Kenneth Eugene (Nick) Knight, a top bronc rider just prior to and during the Second World War. He and Herman appeared at many of the same rodeos, were original members of the Cowboys' Turtle Association and, in Herman's opinion, Knight was "one of the best." He was born September 8, 1909 in Creighton, Missouri, but grew up in Cody, Wyoming. Knight married the former Fay Belle Dennis of Rexburg, Idaho, a notable trick rider on the rodeo circuit who had performed with the Gene Autry Rodeo for several years prior to her marriage. Shortly after the war started they took jobs as master welders at a shipyard in Vancouver, Washington and participated in rodeos on a lesser scale. The Knights eventually moved to Beatty, Nevada and purchased a small hotel and casino. They met an untimely death in 1965 while returning from Cody, Wyoming. The small plane

"Badger Mountain" — a scheming demon of bucking destruction.
-Photo courtesy Bob Wiseman and The Ketchpen

Pay Windows Have Increased Since Linder's Rodeo Days

"...I rode White Cloud at Cincinnati and won first prize of $80. Also rode bareback. The show is about to blow up."

- Linder diary, October 2, 1933

"...Rodeo finally blew up. Came home and had supper and played cards."

-Linder diary, October 4, 1933

Walking away from a rodeo pay window with $500 or $1,000 in your jeans in the 1930s meant a cowboy did awfully well in the averages and in the finals.

Rodeos — even the larger ones — were not known for offering large prizes for champions, but in the Depression Years, every little bit helped. And sometimes unscrupulous rodeo promoters would leave town in the midst of a rodeo if they felt they were losing money. The results? Cowboys and stock contractors would have to bear the losses with their entry monies and prize offerings gone and contractors worrying about paying the shipping bill for roughstock to the next rodeo.

This was the case in Cincinnati, Ohio in 1933 when a rodeo producer skipped town midway through performances. Poor crowds indicated there would be a big loss and the producer apparently had neither the stomach nor the purse to ride things through. Many of the contestants sensed things weren't right but were helpless to make any changes.

"We all lost, but at least I was able to pick up my $80 in day money right after the first show. That was a lot of money and allowed Agnes and I to go on to the rodeo in Madison Square Garden in New York," said Herman.

He thinks back to the early years of rodeo and the hand-to-mouth existence that cowboys led.

He recalls the year that Agnes and he arrived in New York in the early 1930s with just $10 left to their name. There were three important items on their "shopping" list: find a place to stay, get some groceries and get entered at Madison Square Garden.

They found a nice housekeeping suite close to the Garden for $10 a week.

"The fellow wanted his money right now and that would leave us without a penny. I said I'd pay him as soon as I won some money at the rodeo," said Herman.

That didn't cut any ice so Herman started to pick up their suitcases. The landlord was going to let him walk. Tears began to fill the eyes of a tired and disconsolate Agnes.

Herman saw he was losing out in two places, turned to the landlord

Herman on Wing at Cheyenne's Frontier Days, 1938.

and asked how would it be if he put $5 down and paid the balance in a couple of days. That turned the tide!

"You can't imagine all the groceries you could buy for $5 in those days and we went on quite a shopping spree," Herman recalled.

There wasn't a dime left to enter the New York rodeo events. Luckily, Herman knew the man at the desk, chose the events he wanted to enter and handed in the list along with a championship watch he had won at an earlier rodeo.

Not a word was said. Fred Alford, rodeo office secretary, scooped up the entry form and watch and placed them both in a drawer.

As things turned out, Herman had no problem reclaiming his watch and paying the balance for the housekeeping suite.

There was also pathos at the New York rodeo.

Herman recorded October 12, 1937: "After tonight's rodeo we closed the arena to crowds and held a funeral for Tuffy Cravens who was killed when tossed by a bull. His casket was in the centre of the arena and the lights were dimmed. We paid our last tribute to him. Took up a collection to send him to his home in Oklahoma. We all felt quite blue."

One who knew the vagaries of the rodeo world was Tom Three Persons of the Blood reserve at Standoff, Alberta. Born March 19, 1888 he worked for various cattle outfits before winning $1,000 first money aboard the saddle bronc Cyclone at the 1912 Calgary Stampede.

Three Persons would later become a successful rancher and in 1934 was running about

Slim Pickens and Saturday Night at the Ranch!

four hundred head of white face cattle and one hundred head of horses.

He was always keen for cowboy contests, saying the only way they can successfully continue, is to offer reasonable purses, with fair entry fees to make it worth a contestant's while, use fair rules, and have only competent and fair judges who will award decisions only upon a fair and square basis, regardless of where a contestant comes from, whether he is a well-known or an unknown.

And the great rodeo clown "Slim Pickens" used his alias to describe the economies of rodeo life. The financial pickings in the rodeo world were indeed slim! He and Herman would become fast friends as Slim worked the rodeos produced by Linder. Prior to his death, Slim found stardom in many Hollywood movies.

And Rodeo Became A Business

"...Rode in the evening at New York's Madison Square Garden and won a beautiful saddle. Got cheques and sent two hundred dollars home."

-Linder diary, October 29, 1933

According to the Professional Rodeo Cowboys Association (PRCA) of the United States, the free-roaming lifestyle of the cowboy shrinks to nearly nothing. But in arenas throughout the land, the spirit of the West lives on through the sport of rodeo.

Rodeo cowboys keep alive the skills of the working cowboy. Tasks such as roping cattle and breaking horses, which were originated and refined by nineteenth-century cowhands, live on today in rodeo competition among modern-day cowboys.

Like schoolboys engaged in arm wrestling contests, early-American cowboys entertained themselves with similar bravado.

"Informal competitions sprang up among cowboys to determine the best ropers and riders. These pasture duels grew so popular that eventually rules were established, then standardized," says the *PRCA Media Guide* for 1996.

And rodeo became a formal sport.

"Of course," says *The Guide*, "the sport has changed dramatically over the years. Some events were dropped and others were added. Animal protection rules have been established. And the award system is overwhelmingly more lucrative than during rodeo's early days.

The tenth annual convention of the Rodeo Association of America was held January 6-7, 1939 in the Murray Hotel, Livingston, Montana. Here's a list of rodeo donors and winners for 1938:

Grand Champion Cowboy: Burel Mulkey, Salmon City, Idaho. $500 cash, presented by Dick Cronin, advertising manager, representing Levi-Strauss Company of San Francisco.

Champion Bronc Rider: Burel Mulkey, Salmon City, Idaho. $200 cash, presented by Harry Rowell, stock contractor, manager of Hayward, Sonora and San Mateo Rodeos.

Directors of the Rodeo Information Commission are seen at a meeting in the Brown Palace Hotel in Denver, Colorado in 1968. Back row, from left: "Doc" Etienne, John Justin, Don Harrington, Gene Pruett, Wally Raymond, Les Connley, H. Edwards, Wes Stetson, Reg Kesler and Skipper Lofting. Front row: Lyn Butler, Bert Kreuger, Wally Sullivan, Gordon Hanson, Herman Linder and T. Fort.

Linder Collection

Champion Bull or Steer Rider: Jud Fletcher, Hugo, Colorado. $100 cash, presented by West-Holliday Company through their representative, Bob Holliday, of San Francisco. Second prize to Hughie Long of Cresson, Texas - $50 cash, also presented by the West-Holliday Company.

Champion Calf Roper: Clyde Burke, Comanche, Oklahoma. $100 cash, presented by the N. Porter Saddle Company of Phoenix and Tucson, Arizona.

Champion Team Roper: John Rhodes, Sombrero Butte, Arizona. $100 cash, presented by H.J. Justin & Son, Fort Worth, Texas. Second prize to Tom Rhodes, $50 cash, also presented by H.J. Justin & Son, makers of Justin Boots.

Champion Steer Wrestler: Everett Bowman, Hillside, Arizona. $100 cash, presented by the John B. Stetson Company, Philadelphia, Pennsylvania, makers of Stetson Hats.

Champion Single Roper: Hugh Bennett, Fort Thomas, Arizona. $250 saddle presented by the Keyston Bros. Saddlery, San Francisco.

Champion Steer Decorator: Warner Linder, Cardston, Alberta, Canada. $100 cash presented by the Howard Automobile Company of San Francisco and Los Angeles, Buick dealers. Second prize to Andy Lund, Milk River, Alberta - $50 cash, also presented by Howard Automobile Company.

Note: The Hamley Saddle Company of Pendleton, Oregon offered $100 in cash to be assigned to some champion for 1939.

The Salant & Salant Company of New York, makers of Uncle Sam Work Shirts, offered $50 for second place in some event for 1939.

The PRCA Guide has this to say about today's rodeo cowboy: "In today's professional rodeo, it is common for a top competitor to win more than $100,000 in a single event in a given year. And cowboys have earned $20,000 to $50,000 from some of the regular season's richest rodeos.

Some rodeo cowboys will travel thousands of miles to compete in more than one hundred rodeos each year.

"Most casual fans know the names of the more-famous cowboys who consistently qualify for the National Finals Rodeo. What those fans don't realize is that most PRCA cowboys hold full-time jobs in other professions and compete in rodeos only part time. Often, their decisions about where

1968 officers and directors of the Rodeo Historical Society. Back row, from left: Eddie Woods, Dean Krakel, Herman Linder, Hippy Burmeister, Jim Eskew Jr. Front row: Andy Curtis (proxy for Floyd Stillings), Flaxie Fletcher and Phil Meadows.
National Cowboy Hall of Fame and
Western Heritage Center, Oklahoma City photo.

to compete are based on the driving distance to the rodeo and potential earnings.

"While rodeo is a hobby for most PRCA competitors, and a lucrative career for the most skilled, the spirit and traditions defined by those early cowhands are carried on by today's rodeo cowboys."

Approximately 170,000 people attended the National Finals Rodeo in December, 1995, in Las Vegas and more than 1.3 million viewers tuned in to all ten rounds of the Finals on ESPN and ESPN2. It is clear the sport of professional rodeo is growing more popular and competitive than ever.

That growth, says the PRCA, is due largely to the efforts of the

Bart Clennon on a tough one at the Elko, Nevada rodeo.
Bart Clennon photo

Herman, right, receives his Honouree Of The Year Award at Las Vegas, December 10, 1987 from the ProRodeo Historical Society of America. At the mike is Charlie Throckmorton, MC, while Harry Tompkins is on Herman's right. *HG Photo*

association and its eleven thousand members — the largest rodeo-sanctioning body in the world.

In 1995, the association sanctioned 739 rodeos in forty-four states and four Canadian provinces. These PRCA rodeos awarded more than $25.4 million in prize money

PRCA contestants compete in regular season rodeos, striving to qualify for the sport's premier championship event the National Finals Rodeo. In 1995, the NFR offered more than $3 million in prize money.

In addition to contestants, the PRCA is composed of stock contractors, judges, rodeo clowns, bullfighters, secretaries, timers, specialty act performers, announcers and photographers.

The PRCA traces its roots back to 1936 when cowboys staged a walkout at a rodeo at the Boston (Massachusetts) Garden. The protest resulted from the rodeo promoter's refusal to add the cowboys' entry fees to the prize money and to select more qualified judges. (To the best of the author's knowledge, only two of these cowboys are alive today: Herman Linder of Cardston and Bart Clennon of Tucson, Arizona.)

The promoter, Col. W.T. Johnson, finally yielded and the Cowboys' Turtle Association was formed.

In 1945, the Turtles changed their organization's name to the Rodeo Cowboys Association, which in 1975 became the Professional Rodeo Cowboys Association.

In 1987, the PRCA appointed its first commissioner, Lewis A. Cryer, who took office January 1,1988. Since then the PRCA has experienced one of its greatest periods of growth.

The PRCA now employs about sixty full-time people, but the staff grows to nearly one hundred during the peak rodeo season.

The PRCA's national headquarters is adjacent to the ProRodeo Hall of Fame in Colorado Springs, Colorado. A $4.4 million expansion to the Hall was opened in 1996.

The Canadian Professional Rodeo Association says rodeo in Canada was born out of a need by working cowboys for some fun and entertainment — a break from the routine of daily chores on the vast ranches of the Canadian prairies.

"They started out as something like a country picnic," remembers Ken Thomson, who figures the first ones were held in the Alberta communities of Hand Hills and Raymond back around 1902. The former Black Diamond rancher, who now makes his home in Sundre, recalls there were about fourteen or fifteen rodeos around the country through the 1920s, '30s and early '40s. He remembers because he used to compete at them.

The 1996 Official Pro Rodeo Canada Media Guide quotes Thomson in this manner:

"There'd be $10 up in the bronc riding at those smaller shows. Maybe just $5 in the calf roping. They'd pay $3, $2 and $1 for first to third in the bull riding.

"Back in 1934, I entered the bareback riding at a rodeo in Keremeos, British Columbia," recalls Thomson who was

Casey Tibbs and Herman Linder were close friends for many years.
Linder Collection

Statue of ProRodeo Hall of Fame honours the late Casey Tibbs of Fort Pierre, South Dakota, World Champion bronc rider.   *HG Photo*

the first president of the cowboys' association.

"They had one chute, there were no pick-up men and the arena was a patch of ground surrounded by cars and buggies. There was no fence. My horse jumped over the cars and headed into the mountains. I stayed with him for two miles until I got my riggin' off him. I wasn't gonna lose it. I paid $15 for it and that was three months of work back in those days.

"Prize money was practically nothing," Thomson says. "I paid $14 in fees at one rodeo, entering every event. I won four firsts, two seconds and got $34 back."

Professional Rodeo Cowboys Association ProRodeo Hall of Fame.
HG Photo

Thomson says things were pretty bleak back then and that's why cowboys had to organize.

And organize they did, says *The Media Guide*.

The Canadian Cowboys Insurance Association was born in 1944 and three months later, at a Calgary meeting, this became the Cowboys Protective Association. The big need was to create a fund to pay medical bills, but while they were at it, the boys laid down some ground rules for approved rodeos. The minimum purse had to be $100 per event and all entry fees had to go into the prize money. They set standards for arena conditions, hired their own judges, and demanded pick-up men.

Cowboys — about five hundred of them — paid $10 each to be members of the association, which embraced twenty-six rodeos. For the first couple of years, members were assessed an extra dollar on every entry fee to go toward the medical fund.

Since then, the association has grown from a basement operation in a private residence to a centrally-located headquarters in the Stockmen's Centre, a modern, three-storey building near the Calgary International Airport . It has become the Canadian Professional Rodeo Association (CPRA), a governing body of sixty-seven rodeos with a $1 million-a-year operating budget, a membership of seventeen hundred and prize money that is expected to exceed $3 million in 1996.

Past presidents include: Ken Thomson, Cliff Vandergrift, Brian Butterfield, Dick Havens, Tom Butterfield, Gid Garstad, Malcolm Jones, Norman Edge, Bob Robinson, Phil Doan, Lynn Jensen, Lee Phillips, Bob Robertson and Jim Dunn. The 1996 president is Drake Whitney.

In its initial year, the Canadian Finals Rodeo in Edmonton attracted 24,499 patrons and awarded prize money of $29,478. In 1995, attendance was 83,458 and total purses were $392,280.

All-Around Cowboy Champion for 1995 was Duane Daines, of Innisfail, Alberta, a three-time All-Around Champion, who was paralyzed from the waist down while competing in the saddle bronc event at Armstrong, British Columbia, in September, 1995.

According to Dwayne Erickson, rodeo columnist for the *Calgary Sun* (October 12/96) prize money for the CFR has shot up more than $90,000 over 1995 to a total of $483,000.

The increase is the result of a new five-year agreement between the CPRA and Edmonton Northlands that kicks in with the 1996 finals.

The portion of the purse contributed by Northlands - $408,000 - is based on 50 percent of gross revenue from the previous year's ticket sales. The remainder of the prize money - $75,000 - comes from sponsors aligned with CPRA.

The sixteen stock contractors who provide the bucking horses and bulls for the finals, also share in the gate revenue and will see their pot rise about $30,000 to $190,000.

Erickson says the hike in prize money - $90,720 - is the second largest in the twenty-two year history of the finals. It was exceeded only by a $107,000 jump in 1990.

As *The Media Guide* says so eloquently, the country picnic has become a major business organization.

When the Canadian group started, Linder was on the other side of the fence. He had turned from cowboy competitor to rodeo manager. But he never forgot those tough early days of rodeo and its a credit to his fair dealings that he is a life member of both American and Canadian associations.

Herman Linder went from cowboy contestant to rodeo manager and arena director.
Linder Collection

Cardston Rotarians Honour Linder

It was a proud day for a modest man, January 22, 1934, when the Cardston Rotary Club held a civic reception for the community's cowboy hero. More than two hundred and fifty were in attendance.

Mayor Burt, representing the town, presented Herman with an engraved watch fob from the Rodeo Association of America (RAA) for his rodeo standings in 1933. This included second place in bareback, third in bull riding and third in the All-Around.

D.O. Wright, Rotary president, introduced Charlie Cheesman, veteran secretary of the Cardston Athletic Association.

"I consider it an honour to be the guest speaker at a dinner honouring a man who is ranked as a world champion in his particular line of endeavor.

"Herman is known and liked by every stockman and cowhand on the American continent: Calgary, Pendleton, New York, Cheyenne, Boston and especially, here at home in Cardston," Cheesman said.

He spoke eloquently of Herman's rodeo history and concluded with these words:

"This quiet, unassuming boy has done more to advertise the town of Cardston and the province of Alberta than any other man in his particular line."

Chairman of the dinner was Sylvester W. Low, with plenty of singing including *Hold Your Horses.*

It was some years before the RAA, formed in 1929, would recognize its champions with more than a watch fob or pearl-handled pocket knife (Herman has three.) The latter was given for being among the ten top contestants in North America in the mid-1930s.

Cardston Rotarians held a civic reception in 1934 for their hometown boy who won fame in the rodeo infield. Glenbow Archives NA-3252-4

Old Wine In New Bottles

"...I was with Nick Knight and Burel Mulkey and we played pool at Indianapolis. My bareback horse bucked me off. Feel terrible over the riggings we have to use to ride."

—Linder diary, September 25, 1935

Nick Knight

Is rodeo different today than it was sixty years ago? Quite probably, according to Herman.

"The horses were a little tougher in those days because they weren't hauled so far and there were more to choose from. We'd get them grain fed and full of fight. Green broncs will usually fire hard the first time and they may never fire again. There were a lot of them, and they weren't even halter broke, some were bad-mannered in the chute and fought you all the way.

"Yesterday's bronc riders were just as good as the ones today, but no better. They spurred their saddle broncs just as hard and high as they do in 1996, but I think the bareback rider today spurs a lot higher and wilder than they did years ago.

"There was a time, we were allowed to use our own saddles and riggings, and then the rodeo bosses decided everyone should use a standard tree, so they introduced the Association saddle in the mid-1920s, and it's been with us ever since.

"I remember when we rode in New York in the 1930s they had ten chutes — all numbered — and they had ten Association saddles with corresponding numbers. If you drew a horse that wound up in chute eight, you used the saddle marked eight. The same with the bareback riggings. The next day you might pull a horse that stood in chute one, so you changed saddles again.

"Nowadays, the boys use a lot of resin and other sticky stuff that would have gotten you disqualified years ago. In earlier days, the breaks all went to the stock.

"I believe the professional cowboy associations have changed many things for the better for the rodeo contestant and the sport in general, starting with the Cowboy Turtles. I'm glad I played a small part in helping to improve the lot of the cowboy."

Pardner Was Their Nemesis

"...Made a good ride here at Boston on Old Pardner whose now called Schoolboy Rowe. I think the old horse remembered me."

—Linder diary November 2, 1937

The horse's name was *Pardner Brown*, alias *Schoolboy Rowe*, a black gelding that could turn on a dime and give you some change. A horse the Linder brothers, Herman and Warner, tried to ride out of their side chute at the ranch, and never quite succeeded.

Pardner came over to the Linders when their dad traded ten weaner pigs for the two-year-old black colt so his boys could have a bucking horse to practice on. Neighbours said the horse could really buck. This proved to be an understatement.

"Pardner loved to buck!" Herman recalled. "Put a regular form-fitter saddle on him and we could ride him without much trouble. But as soon as we rigged him with our Association saddle with its thirteen-inch tree, it was another story and one that always had the same rough ending. We tried him with that competition saddle every day for two weeks — both of us — and each time we hit the dirt.

"When he bucked us off we would bring him in and give him a feed of oats. It got so that every time he dumped us he'd come running to the corral on his own, looking for that feed. I guess he figured he had done his part and now he wanted his reward."

Herman and Warner decided this was a bronc they couldn't master and if an old farm horse could toss them, how could they ever become rodeo stars? They gave up the idea of being rodeo hands and used Pardner to herd cattle and, later, put him to work as a draft horse.

In a few years time, a rodeo was being held in Cardston and brother Warner asked stock contractor Ray Knight if he could use another saddle bronc.

"Sure," said Knight, "but he's gotta be good."

"I'll bring you one that will toss every rider that gets on him. If he does, pay me $5. If he's ridden, you don't owe me a dime," said Warner.

Herman drove the farm pick-up while Warner rode Pardner the six miles into town. He dismounted, took the saddle off Pardner, and tossed it in the back of the truck.

Knight fumed and fussed as Warner turned Pardner in with the other rodeo horses. He was a former bronc buster, but it bothered him that someone would ride an "untamed outlaw" into the arena for all to see.

No one could ride Pardner at Cardston, including Slim Watrin of High River, a rider of renown who won the bronc riding at Calgary in 1928 and again in 1931.

From left: Lawrence Watrin, Herman, Norman Edge and Einar Brasso at the annual salute to the Old-time Cowboys at Rotary House during the 1995 Calgary Stampede. In 1929, Edge won the Wild Horse Race at the Calgary Stampede; in 1925, he was bareback champion; in 1927, he won the bullriding; and in 1928, he repeated as bareback champion. Born Norman Frank Edge, June 12, 1904, in the Cochrane, Alberta area, he was one of several Alberta cowboys to participate in a Rodeo in London, England, in 1934. He was inducted into the Canadian Rodeo Hall of Fame November 9, 1983 and passed away in March, 1996 at the age of ninety-two years. HG Photo

Herman sold Pardner in 1934 to Colonel W.T. Johnson, a prominent rodeo producer for $250 with the proviso he'd be paid once the horse had proven himself as a top rodeo mount. Pardner, now School Boy Rowe, would later be listed as one of the twelve best bucking horses in the USA rodeo circuit. After the 1935 World Series Rodeo at Madison Square Garden, the horse had been ridden just three times. But no money was forthcoming.

Badly injured by Big Boy, a bay saddle bronc in Boston in November, 1935, Herman needed money for hospital bills and asked wife Agnes to see the Colonel and collect for Pardner. He reluctantly handed over $100 and said Herman would get the balance when the horse had proven himself.

One year later, the cowboys went on strike at Boston Garden for a bigger purse and inclusion of their entry fees in that purse. While the strike was on, Boston Garden manager, George B. Brown, had thrown open the books to the strikers to show that the Garden didn't make a big killing on rodeos.

Examining the previous year's disbursements, the cowboys came across an item that read: "Herman Linder, $100." Brown explained that he gave the money to Johnson to help with Herman's hospital expenses when he was hurt in 1935.

When Herman tackled the Colonel about it, he exploded, saying Herman got the $100.

"That $100 was a downpayment on Pardner," Herman responded. But the Colonel said $100 was $100. Between the gift from the Garden and the sale of Pardner, Herman ended up $250 short. And he always felt this was another reason the Colonel quit producing rodeos at the end of the Boston strike. The cowboys knew what the Colonel had tried to do to Herman while their pal was flat on his back from injuries. Herman got nothing for his horse, $100 through the generosity of Boston Garden and Colonel Johnson would never produce another rodeo.

Herman's last encounter with Pardner was at Boston in 1937. He drew him at Chute No. 6 and gave the gelding's forelock a gentle rub before lowering himself into the saddle. The gate swung open and Herman made one of the rides of his life aboard his old friend. The crowd roared its appreciation as Herman was lowered to the ground by a pick-up man.

It was a hot Independence Day rodeo at Kalispell, Montana, July 4, 1940 and it got even hotter. A railbird was questioning Herman's decisions as a rodeo judge all afternoon – until Herman could take no more. The cowhands gathered 'round as Herman, back to camera, hung a good one on his critic. Photo Art Shop, Kalispell, photo.

Rodeo stock contractor Leo Cremer and Sally Rand are seen at Great Falls, Montana during rodeo days. Early on, Sally was known for her fan dancing abilities, but she's well covered here. Doubleday photo

Rodeo Judge And Horse Buyer

"...At Stettler (Alberta) rodeo buying bucking horses when Agnes sent a telegram that I was a daddy. Mother and son George doing just fine."

- Linder diary, June 18, 1942

Herman Linder will be the first to admit that when he stopped competing at rodeos in 1939 he wondered if he could stand life on a ranch without travel or the smell of horseflesh in an arena.

In his last year of rodeo, Herman spent nearly four months on the road, competing in Canada and the United States. As he headed back to Cardston, his cowboy pals all expected to see him back on the rodeo trail come the New Year.

"All of my friends were out there competing and I was at home on the ranch, harvesting, working the cows and pacing the floor," said Herman, who was thirty-two years old at the time.

"Quitin' rodeo was one of the hardest things I ever did. It was awful. If a guy was on dope it would have been just as hard to quit. But I toughed it out."

So Herman took a different tack. With his knowledge of roughstock he began to supply bucking horses for rodeos, shipping broncs out of Canada to the USA to Everett Colborn, Leo Cremer, the Ring boys and Tim Bernard.

His new career began when Herman attended a meeting of rodeo managers at Salinas, California in 1941. He had a long conversation with stock contractor Leo Cremer and they made a deal that turned Herman loose to find a carload of bucking horses for United States rodeos.

Whether judging rodeos at Stettler, Alberta or Kalispell or Great Falls, Montana, Madison Square Garden in New York, Cheyenne, Wyoming, Pine Lake, Alberta or Ellensburg, Washington — or as a spectator at the Calgary Stampede, Herman kept an eye out for good bucking broncs.

It got to the point that Herman could supply more broncs than Cremer needed. Enter Everett Colborn, a noted stock contractor, whose influence and interest in rodeo spanned the continent. He told Herman to go ahead and buy all the broncs he could find. But they couldn't see eye-to-eye on price and Colborn said thanks, but no thanks to using Herman's horse smarts. He'd see to Canadian horse purchases on his own!

Always the entrepreneur, Herman drew up a contract offering horse owners a small down payment and first option for Herman to buy the horse within a specified period of time. He packed the contract everywhere, getting signatures where a horse showed potential for bucking.

When Colborn came to Canada during the summer rodeo circuit, he quickly discovered the horses he liked were "under contract." A smart businessman in his own right, Colborn quickly came to terms with Herman and told him: "I'll buy all the horses you recommend," and "I'll see that cowboy movie star Gene Autry appears at your next rodeo." (Autry was an early business partner of Colborn in staging rodeos.)

"...We met Gene Autry, Everett Colborn and Harry Knight at the Lethbridge airport. Cocktail party and dinner."

- Linder diary, July 3, 1946

Colborn was true to his word on both counts and this led to a long and friendly business relationship between the two men.

Herman's knowledge of rodeo stock is impressive. Following his active career, he ran and produced many Canadian rodeos where he would supply the rough-string horses. He probably shipped more broncs out of Canada than all others put together. Chief Tyhee and Bear Park were two double-rank horses that went to Colborn. (Chief Tyhee is honoured on the Trail of Great Bucking Horses.)

These two horses and many others, came from Long Time Squirrel, a member of the twelve-hundred-section Blood Reservation who owned nearly five hundred head. When Long Time Squirrel died, the part of the

Cowboy singing star Gene Autry shakes hands with four-year-old George Linder at Lethbridge.   Linder Collection

> "...The peak year of my life financially. Shipped twenty-two bucking horses across the line. Had a big rodeo in Lethbridge with *Gene Autry* the entertainment attraction."
>
> *- Linder diary, December 31, 1946*

Skilfully and artfully, Herman Linder combined rodeo judging and horse buying into a business form that allowed him to mix with cowboys, rodeo managers, stock contractors and horse breeders. It was the old days all over again, with the physical punishment of rodeo absent.

> "... We had to go on parade to New York City Hall today. The rodeo started tonight and I judged the first show of my life and the largest in the world. I'm grateful to Col. Kilpatrick of Madison Square Garden for giving me this chance."
>
> *- Linder diary, Oct. 5, 1939*

The Cardston ranch claimed much time as Herman and Agnes developed their cow herd and planned their first residence on the home quarter, after seven years in a one-room log cabin. He would joyfully write they would spend their "first night in our nice new home and in our nice new bed" on November 29, 1939. And they connected the lights and "enjoyed electricity for the first time on December 19 of that same year.

Father Herman Sr. and mother Marie and brother Warner were all engaged in the farm/ranch enterprise and on January 9, 1941, Herman recorded that he and Warner wired the barn "and tonight is the first electricity we have enjoyed there."

Herman carries many memories of his rodeo judging and horse buying days, most of them happy ones, some with a touch of sadness.

> "...Judging rodeo at Great Falls today but a great tragedy happened. Two planes crashed killing six people, burned a race barn with nineteen race horses."
>
> *- Linder diary, August 9, 1946*

Cowboy contestant, rancher, horse buyer and rodeo judge, the stage was now set for Herman Linder Rodeo Enterprises Ltd. — the management and direction of several Canadian rodeos.

Canadian government under Indian Affairs forced his estate to sell the entire band of horses. In 1946, horses were only worth twenty-five cents a pound at the most. So, to insure not being outbid, Herman offered about $10 a head higher than he figured his competition would bid. The horses were branded Lazy B169.

Knowing the Blood people were upset with the forced sale of the horses, Herman donated fifty head back to the tribe as a gesture of goodwill, something the Indian men and women never forgot.

A CORDIAL INVITATION TO A MIGHTY CELEBRATION IN THE TEMPLE CITY OF CANADA

JUNE 28-29-30-   JULY 1-2-3-

Cardston Golden Jubilee.

1887   CARDSTON   ALBERTA   1937

THE GREATEST HOME-COMING EVER STAGED IN ALBERTA

CARDSTON, ALTA.,
CANADA

Herman Linder Rodeo Enterprises

"... The Stampede went over well at Cardston, good crowds and good stock. Quite happy with it all."

-Linder diary, July 2, 1937

He was just thirty years of age and still a competitor when Herman Linder was asked to manage Cardston's Golden Jubilee Stampede, billed as "The Greatest Home-Coming Ever Staged in Alberta".

Cardston chairman Mark Coombs, secretary Joseph Card, treasurer Heber Matkin and program and concession manager C.B. Cheesman recognized that Herman had attended many rodeos and could develop an event that would be a credit to the community. They would not be disappointed.

He didn't realize it at the time, but the Cardston invitation carved a new path for Herman, one that would keep him involved in rodeo for the next thirty-two years, 1937-1969, but not as a competitor. Producing and managing rodeos took him from Quebec on the east to Manitoba, Alberta and British Columbia in the west, all under the name of Herman Linder Rodeo Enterprises Ltd.

He had new life pumped into his veins when ranchers and businessmen from Fort Macleod approached him April 19, 1941 and asked him to run their 1942 Midnight Days Stampede — so named for the famous outlaw horse that came

Bareback rider at the Raymond, Alberta Stampede.

*Photo courtesy
M. Heggie, Raymond*

81

The late Dan Boyle presents Herman with an Honourary Citizen scroll from the Town of Fort Macleod for Herman's longtime involvement in the stampede in that centre.   Lethbridge Herald photo

from the Fort Macleod area. Their agreement would last for twenty-five years and result in Herman being made an Honourary Citizen of Fort Macleod and an Honourary Member of the Fort Macleod Rotary Club. This would also be the site of his most serious rodeo injury in July, 1967. He was sidelined for a number of weeks after a riderless, bareback horse crashed into his mount in the Fort Macleod infield.

It was in the early 1940s that Herman decided to give both time and energy to making rodeo a professional sport in Canada. For Herman, it was rebirth and a kindling of the spirit.

"... Record crowd at Fort Macleod rodeo. Everyone satisfied."

- Linder diary, July 1, 1942

"... Cardston parade and rodeo went off swell. Weather fine and a good crowd.

- Linder diary, July 15, 1942

During the 1930s a loose association of southern Alberta stampedes had been formed. According to *Canadian Rodeo News*, the purpose was to purchase five association saddles and bareback riggings. In those days it was one of the rules that each rodeo furnished the saddle and the riggings at individual rodeos including Raymond, Lethbridge, Claresholm, Carmangay and Cardston. These were purchased and moved from show to show until all five rodeos were over, then stored until the following season. This was discontinued sometime in the 1940s.

The Medicine Hat Stampede has always been close to Herman's heart. He's seen in conversation with the late Dirk Scholten, left, longtime Stampede manager, and Rod Carry, right, Medicine Hat Stampede president 1973-1974.   McCorkle photo

Herman visits with Bert Gibb, right, of Cardston, who faithfully kept the records for the Southern Alberta Rodeo Circuit for twenty years. *HG Photo*

Midnight Days Stampede is no more at Fort Macleod and weeds occupy the spaces where fans once sat. *HG Photo*

According to *The News*, it was 1939 before any cash or award was made by the southern group, which was $250 for the All-Around champion at season's end. Not surprisingly, Herman Linder was the winner.

Following the Second World War, rodeo took on a new dimension in Canada. Communities such as Medicine Hat got stampede fever and started anew with a rodeo that had been dormant for many years. Stockmen such as Henry Cavan, Gene Burton, Lorne Thompson and Mac Higdon and businessmen like Dirk Scholten, Rube Gardner, Harry Hutchings and Hop Yuill asked Herman to be their stampede manager and arena director in 1947.

A rodeo meeting was held at Fort Macleod January 28, 1947, chaired by P.C. Dougherty of High River and the Southern Alberta Rodeo Circuit was formed at that time. Dan Boyle of Fort Macleod was elected president and Jim Burke of the same community elected secretary with representatives from the eight towns present (Nanton, Lethbridge, Claresholm, Fort Macleod, High River, Coleman, Cardston, Medicine Hat) elected as directors. Bert Gibb of Cardston would be named circuit secretary in 1950 and faithfully kept the records for the next twenty-two years.

Purposes of the circuit were to: set dates for rodeos, develop better shows, further cooperation between towns holding rodeos and for cooperative advertising and entertainment.

During the 1940s, Herman Linder began acting as arena director of many of the circuit rodeos. He had the responsibility for contracting stock, hiring rodeo help such as pick-up men and arena help, looking after the rodeo office, printing daily programs, hiring clowns and rodeo acts which could be used at the different rodeos, and seeing that events ran smoothly in the arena. Helping for many years were stock contractor Reg Kesler of Rosemary, Alberta and announcer Warren Cooper of Nanton, Alberta.

At a 1948 meeting in Fort Macleod, directors felt there should be a trophy and $100 cash for winners of each event and the All-Around title. Albert Swinarton of Fort Macleod, Bob Kitson of Lethbridge and Herman formed a committee to explore what might be done.

They were successful beyond measure. Several firms gave $400 towards a hand-tooled saddle and $200 prize money for each event: Calgary

Brewing and Malting Co., Calgary Power Co., Sick's Lethbridge Brewery, Canadian Western Natural Gas, Standard Gravel and National Paving, Greyhound Lines of Canada and Valley Feeders of Lethbridge. Eventually, Eamor's Saddlery of High River sponsored the ladies' barrel racing.

The saddles were the first given out for the various events in Canadian rodeo and along with the generous cash prizes of $200 helped to attract top competitors from both sides of the line. The late Bob Duce of Cardston won ten saddles and Tom Bews of Longview, Alberta, eight to set the cowboy pace.

The southern circuit was the launching pad for many of Herman's ideas on rodeo improvement. He replaced steer decorating with steer wrestling in 1950. It is noteworthy that steer decorating was held at the Calgary Stampede until 1966 when Stan Walker of Lethbridge was the winner. Steer wrestling followed in 1967 and the winner was Roy Duval of Oklahoma.

Herman introduced ladies' barrel racing in 1962 and held the first Miss Rodeo Canada contest in 1955. Winner Connie Ivins of Cardston later competed for the Miss Rodeo America title at Casper, Wyoming that same year.

Because of rodeo horse dealings with Everett Colborn, Herman was able to feature cowboy singing star Gene Autry at the July 3, 1946 Lethbridge Stampede. And rodeo clown sensation Slim Pickens attended many Linder rodeos because of the mutual respect each held for the other. They were also fast friends.

The late rodeo clown and movie star Slim Pickens was a great friend of the Linder family.
Linder Collection

SADDLE
SADDLE

1970	TOM BEWS	①
1969	TOM BEWS	⑥
968	TOM BEWS	⑧
967	KENNY MCKEAN	✓
1966	ROCKEY ROCKABAR	✓
1965	JACK PHIPPS	✓
1964	TOM BEWS	④
963	GEORGE MYTON	✓
962	LEO BROWN	✓
961	ARON PORSKEY	✓
1960	KEITH HYLAND	✓
1959	KENNY MCKEAN	✓
1958	KEITH HYLAND	✓
957	ALVIN OWINS	✓
956	ALVIN OWINS	✓
955	FRANK DUCE	✓
954	CARL OLSON	✓
953	ELLIE LAWIS	✓
952	FRANK DUCE	✓
951	FRANK DUCE	✓
950	CARL OLSON	✓
971	ROCKEY ROCKABAR	

Bare Back	Brahma Bull	Roping	Wrestling	Barrel Racing	All-Around	Trophy Saddle Winners		Statistics by Bert Gibb Cardston, Alta.	
Malcolm Jones ①	Dale Fuhrman ✓	Joe Lowrence	Arnold Haraga	Joy Duck	Tom Bews ⑤	Bob Duck	10	Jack Phipps	1
Malcolm Jones ②	John Dodds ✓	Howard Buttons	Benny Raynolds	Isobel Miller	Tom Bews ⑥	Tom Bews	8	George Myron	1
Malcolm Jones ③	Gid Garstad ✓	Bill Lawrence	Dave Penner	Geraldine McLaughlin	Tom Bews ⑦	Rockey Rockabar	4	Aron Pursley	1
Dick Havens ✓	John Dodds ✓	Kenny McKean	Harold Manderville ②	Joy Duck	Kenny McKean ✓	Bud Vanclevur	5	Ellie Lewis	1
Bob Duck ①	Gid Garstad ✓	Jerry Koike	Tom Butterfield ✓	Joy Duck	Rockey Rockabar	Bud Butterfield	6	George Akdoff	1
Bob Duck ②	Dave Garstad ✓	Jerry Koike	D.C. Lund	Jerri Duck	D.C. Lund	Tom Butterfield	1	Bill Johnson	1
Malcolm Jones ④	Lawrence Hutchson	Ernst Forestburg	Bud Butterfield ✓	Jerri Duck	Tom Bews ⑧	Gid Garstad	3	Don McLeod	1
Bob Duck ③	Gid Garstad ✓	Lorna Wells	Roy Hubbard	Jerri Duck	Kenny McKean ✓	Leo Brown	4	Eddie Akridge	1
Bob Duck ④	Lawrence Hutchison ✓	Emil Chomistic	Bud Butterfield ✓	Echo McCarrey	Dick Havens	Alvin Owens	66	Red McDowell	1
Bob Duck ⑤	Leo Brown ✓	Fred Gladstone	Bud Butterfield ✓		Bob Duck ⑨	Malcolm Jones	4	Charlie Chick	1
Alvin Owens ✓	Wilf Garlitz ✓	Ervin Carlson	Harold Manderville ③		Harold Manderville ③	Kenny McKean	5	Dale Fuhrman	1
Dick Havens ✓	Leo Brown ✓	Buddy Vanclevur ①	Bud Butterfield ✓		Bud Vanclevur ③	Keith Hyland	2	John Dodds	2
Brian Butterfield ✓	Leo Brown ✓	Cliff Vandergriff	Bud Butterfield ✓		Bud Vanclevur ④	Frank Duck	3	Dave Garstad	1
Brian Butterfield ✓	Wilf Garlitz ✓	Gordon Hall	Bud Butterfield ✓		Alvin Owens ✓	Carl Okson	2	
Alvin Owens ✓	Benny Raynolds ✓	Byron Wolford ✓	Harold Manderville ④		Alvin Owens ✓	Dick Havens	3	
Bill Johnson ✓	Dick Bryant ✓	Buddy Still ✓	Paul Templeton		Paul Templeton ✓	Brian Butterfield	2	
Don McLeod ✓	Steve Johnson ✓	Byron Wolford	Bud Vanclevur ①		Bud Vanclevur ⑤	Harold Manderville	5	
George Akdoff ✓	Dan Templeton ✓	Bill Collins	Bill Collins		Bill Collins ✓	D.C. Lund	2	
Bob Duck ⑥	Buddy Heaton ✓	F.C. Stover	Bob Duck ⑧		Bob Duck ⑩	Bill Collins	3	
Bob Duck ⑦	Harold Manderville ⑤	Jack Morton	Larry Reinay ✓		Eddie Akridge ✓	Paul Templeton	2	
Charlie Chick ✓	Red McDowell	Fred Gladstone	Padget Berry		Red McDowell ✓	Lynn Jensen	2	
Lynn Jensen			Rockey Roka	Geraldine McLaughlin	Lynn Jensen	Lawrence Hutchins	2	

Southern Alberta Rodeo Circuit Winners 1950 - 1971

Winners of the Southern Alberta Rodeo Circuit 1950 - 1970 by Secretary Bert Gibb

Southern Alberta Rodeo Circuit

GRAND PRIZES — CASH AND TROPHIES — $2,400.00
Donated By

Calgary Brewing & Malting Co.	Sick's Lethbridge Brewery
Calgary Power Company	Standard Gravel & National Paving
Canadian Western Natural Gas	Western Canada Greyhound

Herman always had a high profile as arena director and his silver mounted saddle won a lot of attention.   *Linder Collection*

Relationships were not always harmonious between a rodeo producer and boards of directors. Herman was cut to the core when the Edmonton (Alberta) Exhibition board dispensed with his services after a ten-year period.

Former El Rancho Motor Hotel owner Mel Fengstad seemingly ruled the roost at the Lethbridge Stampede and was determined that rodeo clown Slim Pickens would not appear at Medicine Hat in 1964, only at Lethbridge, even though Herman had worked out an equitable financial arrangement for the two rodeos. For some reason, Fengstad was prepared to pay Pickens to do a solo appearance at Lethbridge. The Medicine Hat Stampede won out, and Pickens appeared there. Fengstad later severed Herman's Lethbridge contract.

The motel owner later moved to the West Coast where he died in a home accident. In 1976, another Lethbridge fair board had Herman open their annual rodeo and inducted him into their Agricultural Hall of Fame.

Working from his Cardston base, he expanded to produce rodeos in many centres: Penticton and Vancouver, British Columbia; Winnipeg, Manitoba; Montreal, Quebec; the Rodeo of Champions in Edmonton and an expanding Southern Alberta Rodeo circuit.

Herman believed a rodeo should be filled with action from start to finish, no delays at the chutes and the ranker the stock the better. He was fair in his dealings and courtly in his bearing.

As an individual, he was among the first in the design, production and promotion of rodeo in Canada. He was a go-getter and a pacesetter. As an individual boosting the sport of rodeo, he had no equal.

Tragedy In The Barn

"... Finished hauling all the wheat at Staples. Left truck in town and brother Warner brought me home. When we arrived we found our father dead. Terrible. Terrible."

—Linder diary, July 30, 1943

Herman Linder, Sr.
Linder Collection

Fate is how Herman described it.

At a time when he should have been judging the rodeo at Frontier Days in Cheyenne, Wyoming, Herman was at home, assisting his brother with funeral arrangements for his sixty-three-year-old father, the victim of a skull fracture in a fall from the hayloft.

It was during the Second World War and Herman was to catch a plane from Lethbridge, Alberta to Cheyenne. For some reason, the plane did not arrive, so Herman boarded a bus for Great Falls, Montana.

"...Called airline at 9 a.m. and they told me I could only go as far as Billings, Montana which was too late to catch train or bus. Called Cheyenne with my regrets and came home. Felt very blue."

—Linder diary, July 26, 1943

For the next few days, Herman was engaged in hauling wheat, and then, on that fateful July 30, the two brothers drove into the ranch yard to find their mother Marie in tears and pointing towards the barn. "Your father! Your father!" she screamed.

It was haying time and there they found their father, who, just minutes before, had plunged down an opening in the loft. He struck his head in the fall and was killed instantly.

As was the custom, the senior Linder was taken to Cardston, prepared for viewing and funeral arrangements were made. He was returned to the ranch for a day so that friends and neighbours could come and pay their respects at the residence.

"They brought our daddy back. We had many people come to see him and we felt a little happiness to have him home," said Herman's diary entry of August 2, 1943.

But the pain remained. "Took daddy to the service, then to the graveside. Broken heart," reads his diary for August 3, 1943.

Marpole Rotarians and Herman, standing eighth from left, are ready for their 1949 Stampede in Vancouver.
Linder Collection

"...Went to the court house early and got first case thrown out."
- *Linder diary June 2, 1949*

"...Went back to the court house and lost the last case. Felt bad and there was terrible publicity."
- *Linder diary, June 3, 1949*

"...Our case came up in Victoria this a.m. Finished about 3 p.m. Things don't look too good. Feel very blue."
- *Linder diary, February 6, 1950*

Showdown At Vancouver

For Herman Linder, Vancouver, British Columbia represented the best of times and the worst of times in rodeo.

In 1949, 1960, and again in 1969, Herman would ride the roller-coaster of success and failure and feel the wrath of public opinion and the knee-jerk reaction of a hostile court. Herman emerged with his character intact and the future of rodeo assured in Canada, but he had to go all the way to the Appellate Division of the Supreme Court of British Columbia to win the day and thousands of dollars were lost along the way.

At the start, the Marpole Rodeo was hailed by a newspaper as "The Biggest Rodeo Vancouver has ever seen." Another paper called it the "Sixth largest rodeo on the Continent." There were the well-known cowboy events, clowns, Slim Pickens and his famous bullfighting act and a girls' drill team from Seattle. The Rotary Club's rodeo committee, which was headed by Nat Bailey — famous for his White Spot restaurants — was confident this would be the biggest and best stampede ever to come to Vancouver.

It was certainly the most highly publicized. The show began with a near riot because of a misunderstanding about the tickets. Many people failed to read the instructions on stubs bought from street and store vendors which read: "Please exchange stubs for reserve seats by mailing, or present same to Hick's Ticket Bureau, 610 Dunsmuir Street."

Thousands of eager fans had to be turned away after waiting in line for as long as two hours because there was not enough space to handle them. While about eight thousand people jammed the seats inside, another ten thousand stood outside demanding to get in. Several scuffles broke out in the two-block-long lineup the first afternoon. Headlines screamed: "Huge Crowd Misses Stampede" and "Ten Thousand Irate as Doors Shut."

For Herman, in 1949, Vancouver represented the first opportunity to stage a rodeo in a major Canadian City. His happiness knew no bounds when he signed a contract with the Marpole Rotary Club to stage a four-day rodeo, May 24-28, at Callister Park in Vancouver's East Hastings district, located just west of the city's main Exhibition Grounds

Prize money of $7,800 and six trophy saddles would be available to contestants who included Floyd Peters, Ken Brower, Carl Olson, Homer Pettigrew, Bill Linderman, "Wag" Blessing, Vern Goodrich, Harold Mandeville, Ed Akridge, Gene Pruitt, Joe Keeler and many others.

Lurking in the shadows were members of the Society for the Prevention of Cruelty to Animals (SPCA), newspaper columnist Jack Scott, and jurists who did little to hide their personal distaste for the rodeo arena.

Cliff Faulknor, in his 1977 biography of Herman Linder, takes the story from here (by permission):

"People who know Herman Linder agree he is both a gentleman and a gentle man. You would have about as much chance of hanging a Cruelty to Animals charge on him and making it stick as you would have making a similar charge against St. Francis of Assisi.

"Nevertheless, such a charge was diligently pursued against Herman in Vancouver in 1949 and was maintained through two courts over a period of a year until the Supreme Court of B.C. finally did what should have been done in the first place — they examined the case on the basis of facts rather than emotion, and threw it out.

"The charge against Herman was pushed by certain elements with the Vancouver branch of the SPCA who thought they saw a chance to keep rodeo out of Vancouver. When a bronc was found with some wounds high on its neck they claimed these were made by spurs and laid the cruelty charge. This was found to be untrue, so they said calf roping was cruel. After that, they attacked the buck strap on broncs. Fortunately, pollution wasn't a big thing in those days, or they might have got him on polluting the arena with horse manure.

"In hindsight, Herman's opponents weren't really after him at all: they were after rodeo itself. Although the charges against Herman were finally

Mr. and Mrs. Harold Mandeville of Skiff, Alberta with Herman in 1995. Mandeville was Canadian All-Around Cowboy at the 1951 Calgary Stampede and Steer Decorating Champion at Calgary in 1957.   *HG Photo*

dropped, so was rodeo as far as Vancouver was concerned. The sponsors of the show decided they'd had enough adverse publicity to last them a lifetime and gave up on the idea.

"But the real trouble was brewing inside where an SPCA inspector had found one of the broncs, *Rimrock*, with some marks on his neck. He reported it to his superiors, and Herman was hauled into the Police Magistrate's Court. There was also testimony that a calf had been thrown to the ground so roughly in the calf roping contest the animal was stunned."

SPCA secretary David Ricardo testified that he saw five marks on *Rimrock's* left shoulder "oozing fresh blood" as the bronc left the arena on May 24, after a ride. *Rimrock* had come right out of the chute bucking with the rider raking from shoulder to flank with the spurs, he said, and a bucking strap was tight under the horse's rear lower belly to make him buck more. He said he had examined the bronc in the corral later with a part-time SPCA inspector named Jim Payne, and had seen the wounds.

Rodeo buffs know a rider has to work his spurs fore and aft or he will lose points. They also know if a rider raked high enough to cause such marks on a horse's neck he would lose his balance and fall off. Later, a veterinarian testified the marks on *Rimrock* were definitely not spur marks — but probably bite marks from another horse.

During the trial, the SPCA claimed *Rimrock* was so seriously injured by the rider's spurs he had to be withdrawn from the contest. Nobody pointed out that, once ridden, a bronc is withdrawn for that Go Round, and another takes it place. At eight seconds or less per ride, bucking horses are used only a few minutes in an entire season.

Rimrock's owner, stock contractor Harold Ring of Wilbur, Washington, denied the bronc had received any spur wounds, insisting *Rimrock* had been bitten by another horse while en route to Vancouver. This was later found to be true when a veterinarian at the Border confirmed the bronc had the marks on him when he entered Canada. A little investigation before the fact would have revealed this, and pre-empted the case.

In the meantime, old *Rimrock* was prancing around Callister Park like a two-year-old, oblivious to the storm being built around him by misguided animal lovers. Unlike his so-called defenders, *Rimrock*, like other new bucking horses, actually lived the life of Riley. As only one horse in a thousand makes a good bucker, such horses are pampered. The average

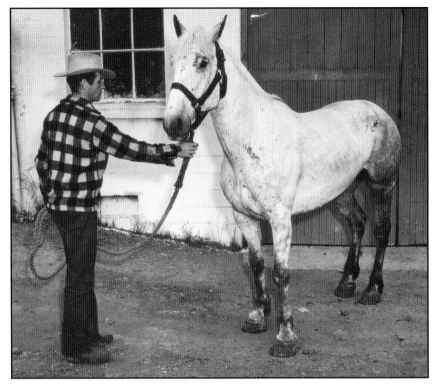

"Rimrock" got lots of publicity at the Vancouver Stampede but it just wasn't deserved.
Linder Collection

age of all broncs in professional rodeo is fifteen to twenty-five years and every major string of buckers has at least one past the age of twenty. In the horse world, this is a ripe old age.

They are also protected from maltreatment by a set of rules produced by the Canadian Rodeo Cowboys Association in conjunction with the national SPCA. But a lot of people don't know this and often react out of emotion rather than knowledge and reason. Some buckers love to buck and do the best they can to unseat their riders, just like a thoroughbred strives to win at the race track.

Police Court Magistrate W.B. McInnes had little sympathy for Herman the rodeo director and fined him $100 or thirty days in jail. The decision was appealed but the case wasn't heard until the following January.

Flushed with victory the SPCA board met to discuss rodeos in general and how to stop them.

They found a fellow traveller in columnist Jack Scott at the Vancouver Province. "Pleasure from torment is the inescapable appeal to the passions that are calculatingly aroused by the rodeo," he wrote.

This prompted a number of letters to city dailies.

"The Rotary Club of Marpole is guilty of the most dishonourable thing of its career in bringing rodeo to Vancouver under its sponsorship. If there is anything on the face of the Earth that is cruel and devilish, it's a rodeo," wrote one.

Said another: "I wonder how many stampede fans have seen the carcass of an animal after it has been in the rodeo arena for a few days? It is not a happy sight."

Incidentally, the dictionary defines "carcass" as the "dead body of an animal or human." And of course rodeo animals don't stay in arenas for days, only a few seconds a few times a week.

But there were others who gave the unhappy Herman and Rotary crew some support.

Said Jean Howarth in the *Vancouver Province*: "Coming from Calgary I watched thirteen Stampedes, and I don't think I ever saw any deliberate cruelty to animals. Unless you would call a cowboy an animal."

Never did a Canadian rodeo show receive such publicity. Never was there so little gain as a result.

The appeal hearing came up before Judge J.C. Lennox in January, 1950 in County Court. Herman was acquitted on the Rimrock charge and also on the charge of cruelty to a calf, and thought he was in the clear, but the court had other plans.

The next thing Herman knew he was defending himself against a charge of using a bucking strap, or flanker, on a horse to make it buck. This was the same type of sheepskin-lined flank strap he had brought back

Herman in his rodeo managing days.
Calgary Herald Photo

from Australia years earlier. It was approved by SPCA branches and Humane Societies for use in rodeos all over the North American continent, but they'd never seen one in Vancouver.

Said *The Vancouver Province* of January 25, 1950: "Rodeo promoter Herman Linder all but saddled himself in Appeal Court today in an attempt to show that the flank strap used on horses at the Rotary Stampede last May could not cause injury. Linder, who has himself won honours in four countries, was appealing a Police Court ruling on abuse of an animal. His detailed description of rodeo techniques supported similar evidence given Monday by Harold Ring of Washington, who had engaged in some heated word battles with Assistant City Prosecutor, Stewart McMorran, who maintained spurs and harness used in bronco busting contests were painful goads."

Judge Lennox brought down his decision February 3, 1950, ruling that flank straps do constitute unnecessary abuse of a horse, and dismissed Herman's appeal from his previous conviction on a cruelty charge. Herman was stunned at the decision and so was the whole rodeo world. This posed a threat to a multi-million-dollar industry, and Herman had plenty of friends to back him when he took the case to the Appellate Division.

"That ruling could not go unchallenged. It wasn't just my fight now. It was an attack against the whole rodeo world."

Herman got in touch with Pinky Baylen of Pendleton, Oregon who was president of the International Rodeo Association, and Baylen assured him he would help in the fight. It was no problem getting the Canadian Stampede Managers' Association to back his cause as Herman was the current president of that group. For good measure, the Cowboys Protective Association, the Calgary Stampede and the Rodeo Cowboys Association also joined the fray. All contributed money to the defence.

Lawyer John L. Farris was engaged to take the case to the Court of Appeal. After careful deliberation, the three appeal judges, headed by Mr. Justice C.H. O'Halloran, reversed the original decision and both Herman and rodeo were vindicated. The prosecution was left without a leg to stand on.

"If a flank strap was a restraint on a horse, so was a saddle cinch," the Appeal Court pointed out. "Did the prosecution figure all saddle horses should be banned too?"

It was April 22, 1950 before the Supreme Court made their ruling and too late for the Marpole Rotary Club to get tickets printed and book space at Callister Park. Plans for the rodeo were cancelled for that year.

"If we had won the first appeal, as we should have, next year's rodeo would've gone on as planned," Herman maintained. "And it would have been a real success because the whole city — in fact, the whole of Canada — was talking about the case. Every time we came to court the place was jammed full. Never did we have such publicity! It was the only rodeo I've ever been to in my life where we had to turn thousands of people away. Inside the park, they were hanging from the rafters."

Pro Rodeo Canada's Media Guide for 1996 listed eleven sanctioned rodeos for British Columbia (including Vancouver) forty-two for Alberta, ten for Saskatchewan and two for Manitoba.

If At First You Don't Succeed. . .

"...Went to exhibition office and got cheques for judges, etc. Had two good crowds. Went to PNE dinner. Busy after last show getting boys paid. Was a fair day."

-Linder diary August 27, 1960

As things turned out, it could have been a fairer day and fairer week.

Herman was referring to the Pacific National Exhibition (PNE) who had asked him to stage a rodeo eleven years after the Callister Park Disaster and to split either the profit or loss. Copious amounts of rain entered the picture and Herman and a few backers dropped fifteen thousand dollars as a result.

As expected, the SPCA urged people to stay away from the rodeo and this turned even one of their own directors against the board. Patrick Burns told his Vancouver branch that the Society had no business trying to keep rodeos out of Vancouver, that it should be concerned only with preventing cruelty to animals, as its name implied.

Newspaper Writer Wilf Bennett, came to the defence of rodeo in his Good Morning column, saying people highly exaggerate any perceived cruelty to animals.

A grateful Herman Linder wrote to Bennett prior to the PNE:

"We who produce rodeos are no more inclined to treat our animals poorly than are you to see this done. Who thinks more highly of his four-legged friend than the man whose livelihood depends on that animal? Rodeo is a part of our North American heritage. It exists only because the cowboys more than any other horse trainer in history, gave the horse an even break. The cowboy on a bucking horse has become a symbol — almost a trademark — of a whole era in North American history.

"Today it is a contest that plays to millions each year. While rodeo action is always violent, it is not dangerous or brutal to animals. You have my pledge that the PNE Rodeo will be carefully conducted under strict regulations."

PNE directors had hopes their rodeo would be a real rival for the Calgary Stampede and would become an annual event.

Between rainfall and another mix-up on the tickets, which caused a lot of people to miss the show, interest in rodeo in Vancouver waned after 1960. The iron was in the fire and what could have been a great yearly show, became nothing but a faded dream.

But there's no telling Herman that rodeo couldn't have succeeded in Vancouver. Never content to say die, Herman and nine friends from Alberta attempted to put on another rodeo in Vancouver in 1969.

"The interest wasn't there and we lost thirty thousand dollars." For Herman, that was the last kick at the cat.

"Perhaps, if we'd been able to go back in 1950 right after we won our case, and then kept coming back, we'd have gotten the job done," he said.

Herman and good friend Warren Cooper of Nanton, Alberta in 1982. "Coop" announced at many rodeos which were managed by Herman.   *Alberta Beef Photo*

Tom and Rosemarie Bews of Longview, Alberta in the garden with Herman.
Alberta Beef Photo

93

Rodeo Sport Of The Wild West

By George Ross, Jr.

Reprinted from the Free Press Weekly Report On Farming, *June 7, 1969 issue. The late George Ross, Jr. of Manyberries, Alberta, was president of the Western Stock Growers' Association from 1962–1965 and his newspaper column was avidly read by stockmen across Western Canada.*

Well the rodeo season is in full swing again and it seems every year the sport gets more popular. I guess it's because it represents one of the few remaining parts of the old west and its glamour.

Much is being said these days about cruelty to animals where rodeos are concerned. In my estimation this is all nonsense. Having operated small Stampedes for some seventeen years, I find these accusations quite uncalled for. In lots of cases I think the animals enjoy the sport as much as the cowboys and spectators. I'd a lot sooner spend my life as a bucking horse than a plow horse or even a saddle horse. They live a pretty soft life if you ask me with just a few minutes hard work in a whole year, whereas the gentle horses have to spend many hours of hard labour in their lives.

Have to look after animals

Although rodeos may seem rough from a grandstand, the rules today pretty well protect the animals from any danger and at these high prices stock contractors just can't afford not to look after their animals in the best possible way. Most of the blood spilled around a rodeo comes from the cowboys, not the stock. When you take a close look behind the chutes, you won't find many spurs sharp enough to scratch an animal's hide and if you look closely, you won't see many cowboys digging their spurs in too deep either. The flank straps aren't cruel, admittedly they make an animal kick but there is usually elastic on them so they'll give enough to let the critter unwind. If they are put on too tight the animal can't move. No, I don't think rodeos can be accused of being cruel to animals.

Rough as football

Rodeo, however, is a rough sport on the contestants, there isn't any doubt about it; next to football it is probably the roughest sport in the world and a lot of people will argue that it is rougher. These fellows who compete in the rough events don't stay in the limelight very long so they have to make their hay while the sun shines. Most suffer for the rest of

Tom Bews of Longview, Alberta aboard a rank saddle bronc.
Linder Collection

their lives from the bumps and bruises and broken bones they get in the rodeo arena. I think bull riding is the roughest of all rodeo events, followed closely by saddle bronc riding, steer wrestling, bareback bronc riding and chuck wagon racing. A cowboy can live a long time in the calf roping and cutting horse events, but they always take some bruising in the wild horse races and wild cow milking competitions too.

Mainly Entertainment

Although rodeos are fast becoming major box office attractions they really don't contribute much to the ranching industry any more like they used to. The fellows who compete are more athletes than cowboys and lots of them wouldn't climb on a bad horse outside of the arena without the pick-up men around. In fact most of the rodeos are held during either the haying season or the branding season when there is a lot of ranch work to be done and the rodeo contestants just aren't there.

It reminds me of what Dad said to a fellow working for him one time: "You know, I think you are one of the best cowmen in the country but you are no good to me if you aren't here."

I enjoy watching a good show and Canada has some of the best bucking horses and the best riders in the world but I'd never advise my son to take up the sport; too many after effects.

The Calgary Exhibition and Stampede commissioned this bronze of Herman by the rodeo sculptor J. Contway. The Stampede board graciously made a gift of a copy of the bronze to the Linder family.
HG Photo

Herman is with Jim Shoulders, left, and humorist Baxter Black, right, at the annual meeting of the Rodeo Historical Society in Las Vegas, Nevada, December, 1995.
HG Photo

Edmonton Was Early Success Story

"...We decided at 7:30 a.m. to move the corrals and chutes into the arena. Worked hard all day with hired help and volunteer cowboys and were ready by night to put the Edmonton show on inside. Cold weather. Show went well."

- Linder diary June 17, 1952

Herman with cowboy champions at Edmonton Rodeo.

Linder Collection

Rodeo producer Herman Linder didn't know it at the time, but a driving Edmonton rainstorm, in June of 1952, would lead to Canada's largest indoor rodeo and later host the nation's largest rodeo purse — the Canadian Finals Rodeo (CFR) each November.

When it became clear there would be no chance of holding a rodeo in Vancouver in 1950, Herman had the chutes hauled to Edmonton, where he had been invited to put on a show. It was to be held at the Exhibition Grounds, just in front of the grandstand, in June, 1951.

Herman acknowledged that few businesses start off making money from the beginning and the Edmonton Rodeo was no exception.

"The first year, we had to hold it outside and it was cool and rained a little. And that wasn't all, we just couldn't get any publicity. In fact, one

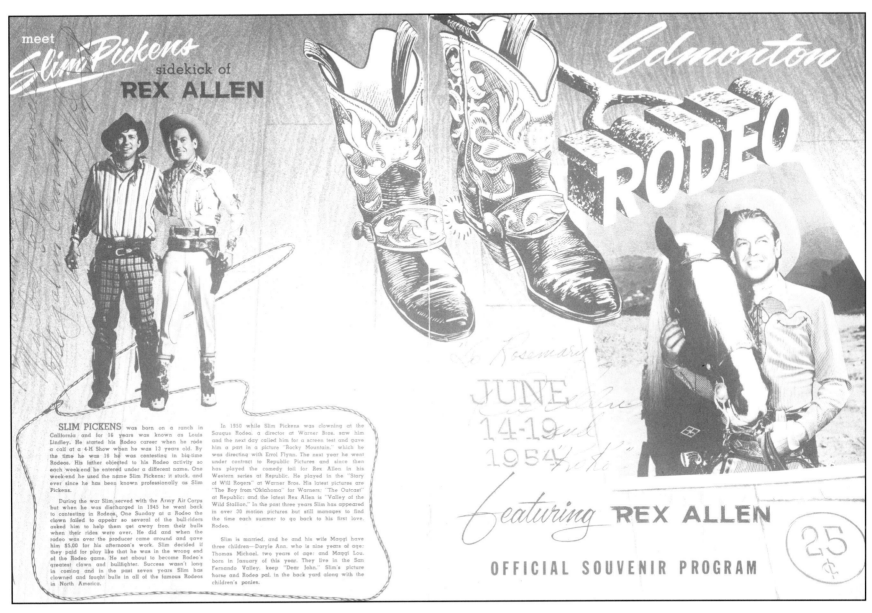

meet
Slim Pickens
sidekick of
REX ALLEN

Edmonton
RODEO

SLIM PICKENS was born on a ranch in California and for 16 years was known as Louis Lindley. He started his Rodeo career when he rode a calf at a 4-H Show when he was 13 years old. By the time he was 16 he was contesting in big-time Rodeos. His father objected to his Rodeo activity so each week-end he entered under a different name. One week-end he used the name Slim Pickens; it stuck, and ever since he has been known professionally as Slim Pickens.

During the war Slim served with the Army Air Corps but when he was discharged in 1945 he went back to contesting in Rodeos. One Sunday at a Rodeo the clown failed to appear so several of the bull-riders asked him to help them get away from their bulls when their rides were over. He did and when the rodeo was over the producer came around and gave him $5.00 for his afternoon's work. Slim decided if they paid for play like that he was in the wrong end of the Rodeo game. He set about to become Rodeo's greatest clown and bullfighter. Success wasn't long in coming and in the past seven years Slim has clowned and fought bulls in all of the famous Rodeos in North America.

In 1950 while Slim Pickens was clowning at the Saugus Rodeo, a director at Warner Bros. saw him and the next day called him for a screen test and gave him a part in a picture "Rocky Mountain," which he was directing with Errol Flynn. The next year he went under contract to Republic Pictures and since then has played the comedy foil for Rex Allen in his Western series at Republic. He played in the "Story of Will Rogers" at Warner Bros. His latest pictures are "The Boy from Oklahoma" for Warners; "The Outcast" at Republic; and the latest Rex Allen is "Valley of the Wild Stallion." In the past three years Slim has appeared in over 30 motion pictures but still manages to find the time each summer to go back to his first love. Rodeo.

Slim is married, and he and his wife Maggi have three children—Daryle Ann, who is nine years of age; Thomas Michael, two years of age; and Maggi Lou, born in January of this year. They live in the San Fernando Valley, keep "Dear John." Slim's picture horse and Rodeo pal, in the back yard along with the children's ponies.

Do Rosemary

JUNE
14-19
1954

featuring **REX ALLEN**

25¢

OFFICIAL SOUVENIR PROGRAM

newspaper was pretty rough on us. Not because they figured rodeo was cruel, or anything like that. They just figured Edmonton shouldn't be doing something Calgary was doing. Edmonton people like to be original, you know."

The first Edmonton Rodeo lost about $6,000. Compared to the Vancouver loss, this wasn't very much, but coming on top of everything, it was enough to cause Herman to do some serious thinking. But Herman Linder Rodeo Enterprises Ltd. stuck to the task and after four years of changing dates around and reshuffling the acts, Edmonton finally began to do well.

Edmonton has hosted the CFR since 1974, paying out $392,280 in prize money in 1995 with a five-day attendance figure of eighty-three thousand four hundred and fifty-eight. This is the largest rodeo purse in the nation, with the Calgary Stampede second at $290,618.

Herman produced the Edmonton show for several years.

"I gambled my own money on it. If the show lost money, I had to pay one third. If it made money, I got a third share of the profits. Of course, after it got going real good and made money steadily, the Exhibition took it over."

Although the show lost a little money that first year, Herman and the Exhibition Association were encouraged to try again in 1952, because the people who attended had shown so much enthusiasm. In spite of the coolness and the drizzle, they lustily cheered each event as it came.

Herman's diary tells of the 1952 rodeo and the start of Canada's largest indoor rodeo.

"...Went out to the Garneau Theatre at 10 a.m. and talked to about 800 children. Was on a radio broadcast at 3 p.m."
- Linder diary June 14, 1952

"Rained some again. Was in the rodeo office taking entries for Warren Cooper."
- Linder diary June 15, 1952

"...Was raining off and on all day. Felt very worried. Made up programs."
- Linder diary, June 16, 1952

Herman has this to say about his diary entries:

"We were in Edmonton well in advance to set up our chutes. It rained continuously for a week and it was still raining the Sunday night prior to the rodeo. Believe me, I never slept a wink. What we lost in 1951 would be peanuts to the $20,000 or $30,000 we would lose with the heavy rain. I was getting sicker and sicker. The stock was there, the ninety-one cowboys had come from all over North America and the acts were ready to go. We would've had to pay the stock contractor and the acts — show or no show.

Norman Edge of Cochrane, Alberta rides a Kesler bull at the March 28, 1974 Edmonton Rodeo.   Linder Collection

"At 4 a.m. I was still pacing the floor and it was still raining. At 6 a.m. I called Jim Paul, then manager of the Edmonton Exhibition Association, at his home and he agreed to meet me at the arena at 7 a.m.

"There was dirt in the Edmonton Gardens as a horse show had taken place some two or three weeks earlier and we were to assess whether there was any possibility of running the rodeo indoors. At 7:30 a.m. we had made the decision to do so, and at 8 a.m. I was downtown at all the radio stations, telling listeners the rodeo would be held indoors. The media couldn't have been more helpful."

Herman recalls that by 9 a.m. about fifty cowboys and ten or twelve of the Exhibition staff jumped in and helped begin the move.

"Without the cowboys we would never have made it, and, of course, they got paid nothing for their troubles.

Hall of Famer cowboy and stock contractor Reg Kesler, right, stood by Herman to help make a success of the Edmonton Rodeo. He's seen with Herman, left, and Shirley Gunderson of Calgary.   *HG Photo*

"The grounds in front of the grandstand were a sea of mud and the only way to move the equipment was to virtually pick it up by manpower and load it on rubber tired buggies.

"How those cowboys worked! They were in mud up to their knees all day long. By 6 p.m. we were set to go, and you know it rained every night of that week. As a matter of fact the roof of the old Gardens had a few leaky spots and we would have to change some of the people over from the seats we had sold them — and we ended up the week with a $2,000 profit," said a happy Herman.

Five thousand people jammed The Gardens and Premier E.C. Manning officially opened the show, paying tribute to producer Herman Linder as "Alberta's outstanding cowboy."

The premier, sporting a western-style white semi-Stetson, said that particularly in Alberta, "where horses romp in the shadow of our drilling rigs, the spirit of the old west is something we will want to keep alive."

Premier Manning commended the Edmonton Exhibition board for its successful change in plans, when, due to the weather, the show had to be moved inside.

"Why shouldn't the rodeo be moved inside? It's held in New York's Madison Square Garden, and what does New York have that Edmonton doesn't have?" asked the premier.

Special guests at the show included famous chuckwagon driver Dick Cosgrave of Calgary and Calgary Stampede founder Guy Weadick of Phoenix, Arizona.

Herman believes Canada's largest indoor rodeo was born of foul weather and, luckily for the City of Edmonton, the rains of 1952 have proven a great boon to the community's economy.

Herman serves wife Agnes a cool drink on the Linder patio. Theresa (Schaab) Harper of Burlington, Ontario and son George Linder are seen in the background.
Alberta Beef Photo

Grand Entry at the Montreal Autostade during Expo '67 in Montreal.

Fred Kobstad Photo

When Howdy Meant Bonjour

"… At last, a nice day. Had over fourteen thousand at matinee and four thousand in eve. Had two performances. The finals of our Great Western Rodeo has come to an end."

—Linder diary, October 15, 1967

Despite cold weather and driving rain and a city-wide transit strike, the Great Western Rodeo held October 6 to 15 at Montreal's Expo '67 turned a profit and added considerable glitter to the fair.

"It was the first rodeo to end up in the black at a World's Fair," said Herman.

Approximately one quarter of a million spectators saw the rodeo, which had a budget of $180,000 and was held in Montreal's Automotive Stadium (Autostade).

When it came to choosing the head man for the Expo '67 rodeo, Herman's name led all the rest. In a letter to John Pratt, deputy director and producer of entertainment, Canadian Corporation for the 1967 World Exhibition, Montreal, Centennial Commissioner John Fisher had this to say: "I understand an old friend of mine, Herman Linder of Cardston, Alberta, is one of the two rodeo producers being considered for your rodeo in Expo's amphitheatre. I have known Herman for many years and he is tops in rodeo productions as far as I'm concerned … you cannot get anybody more knowledgeable. He is a real showman and I think the experts in the business would confirm this."

The late John Fisher was known as "Mr. Canada" and here he was backing a man who was known as Canada's "Mr. Rodeo."

The late Maurice E. Hartnett, former manager of the Calgary Exhibition and Stampede also recommended Herman highly for the job:

"Linder has a good working association with Reg Kesler who is also one of rodeo's outstanding personalities and a Canadian who has won top honours for bronc riding. Linder and Kesler, in my opinion, have access to the best rodeo stock in both the United States and Canada. Each is highly regarded for his reputation as a former contestant … I would not hesitate

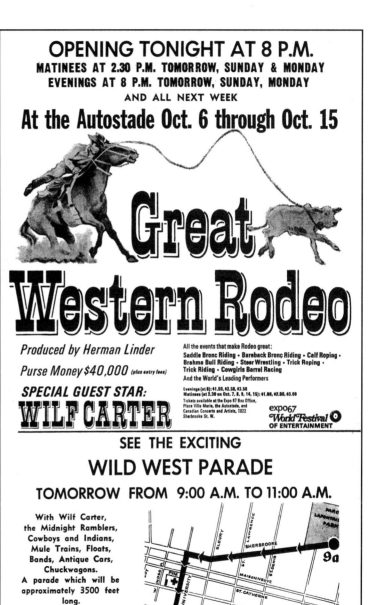

a moment in selecting Linder as your producer. In fact, I feel it would be a great mistake not to do so."

Herman viewed the Expo invitation as the climax to his many years in rodeo. "It was quite a challenge because the complete production of every rodeo phase was in my hands. I was responsible for setting up the chutes and corrals, helping with the advertising, contracting for the stock, and arranging for the freight and feed. I signed all the cheques for every dollar spent on the rodeo."

Twelve Canadian National Railways freight cars were used to ship one hundred and ten broncs, twenty-two Brahma bulls, one hundred and thirty calves and steers and thirty-five saddle horses from Calgary to Montreal.

Herman had to be sharp in his dealings with the railway. He discovered it would cost a lot less to ship the animals to Montreal than to ship them back to Calgary. After much dealing he got an agreement that the same freight rate would be charged both ways.

"It would be amusing if it wasn't so ridiculous," he recalled. "But you know, when we came to ship back, they were still going to charge us this extra money. I had to show them a letter from CN freight officials saying I was to have the same rate both ways before they'd agree to it. The rate they wanted to charge for coming back was one-third more than the rate going down!"

Assisting Herman with the Great Western Rodeo were stock contractor Reg Kesler from Rosemary, Alberta. Fred Kennedy of Calgary handled promotion and publicity. Another pair of top hands were Buster Ivory (stock foreman) and wife June on record-keeping.

Brand Certificate

LINDER & SON RANCH
BOX 1955, CARDSTON
ALBERTA

REGISTERED OWNER OF CATTLE BRAND:

QUARTER CIRCLE H 4
LEFT RIB

H 4

JAN 29 1996

Walter Paszkowski
Minister of Agriculture, Food
and Rural Development

Alberta
AGRICULTURE, FOOD AND
RURAL DEVELOPMENT

This group had a lot to do with the success of the Great Western Rodeo at Montreal in 1967. From left: Herman Linder, producer; Buster Ivory, Texas, stock foreman; Liz and Reg Kesler, Rosemary, Alberta, stock contractor. Not seen is June Ivory, who looked after office management and programming.   HG Photo

The rodeo was held over a ten-day period with fifteen performances, ten in the evening and five in the afternoon. Evening admission was $2.50 and $3.50 while matinee seats were priced from $1 to $3. There was prize money of $40,000 for contestants, a daily grand entry and Wilf Carter (Montana Slim) and the Midnight Ramblers provided nightly western songs with a campfire in the arena. The crowds loved it.

Mayor Jack Leslie and Calgary Exhibition and Stampede Board president A.T. Baker headed up the contingent for Calgary Day at Expo October 6. Montrealers were treated to a downtown "whoop-up" Stampede-style, a monster barbecue and an all-Alberta street parade.

Indian dancers, square dancers, flapjacks and bacon set the mood for two locations: Le Chateau Champlain and Place Ville Marie.

There were other reminders of Calgary including chuckwagons and Stampede Queen Patsy Allen and two Princesses, Candace Smith and Bonnie McGregor.

Alberta Day was held October 7, followed the next day by representatives of the City of Edmonton and the Edmonton Mounted Square Dancers. These were three days Montrealers and world visitors to Expo would long remember.

Gordon Miller, artistic director for Expo's World Festival of Entertainment, would write Herman: "Please accept the appreciation of all of us here, and particularly my personal thanks, for all the creative energy you expended on this project with such great success. Best wishes to you and your colleagues of a fine rodeo team."

As for Herman? His diary would record that he flew to Winnipeg, Manitoba, October 16 and "busy getting ready for the rodeo here."

Wilf Carter with fans and a gold label RCA Victor recording. He's seen at the Horseman's Hall of Fame at the old Calgary Brewery with cowboy pals Dick Cosgrave, Clem Gardner, Herman Linder and Pete Knight. Carter was the main entertainment attraction at the Expo '67 Rodeo.
Linder Collection

Herman Recalls Pete Knight — The Late, Great Cowboy

"We heard of Pete Knight's death today. What a shock for all of us..."

-Linder diary, May 24, 1937

In his book, *We Remember ... Pete Knight*, author Jim Davis of High River, Alberta, wrote:

"To Pete Knight, as to many cowboys of his time, bronc riding was strictly business. As he rode some great bucking horse, the crowd was always sure that they would see a performance becoming a champion. He hailed from the district of Crossfield, Alberta and on October 16, 1976, that community dedicated a new sports arena as the "Pete Knight Memorial Arena."

Pete entered his first rodeo when he was just fifteen and won second in bronc riding. He was plagued by bad luck at his first few Calgary Stampedes. In 1923, the horse he was riding in the Stampede's downtown parade stumbled, fell and broke Knight's leg. The following year, at twenty-one, he missed the Prince of Wales Trophy for bronc riding by a fraction of a point, losing out to fellow Canadian rider, Emery LeGrandeur, in the finals.

"The great rider's career led him to many cities and stampedes. Everywhere he was met with acclaim and praise, as he rose to the world's championship four times before his untimely

death."

The book also carries this article from the July 3, 1937 edition of *The Albertan*, under the heading of "A Tribute to Pete Knight", by the late Guy Weadick, originator of the world-famous Calgary Stampede.

"Along with countless others, I was deeply shocked to learn of the passing of my old friend, Pete Knight. Many have known him since he sprang into prominence as one of the best, if not the leading bronc rider of his day.

"I knew him before he entered the contest arena, that is, when he was running his own outfit in Crossfield with his father and brothers. Not

Pete Knight's Final Ride

It was in 1937, 5:10 that fateful day,
At Hayward, California, on the 23rd of May.

And just to set some people straight on the bronc he rode that day,
It was an outlaw horse named "Duster", that sent him on his way.

The Champ went off that bucking horse and fell beneath his feet,
Old Duster swung back to his left, that's when he trampled Pete.

A broken rib had punctured him as he jumped up on his feet,
Fate had dealt the cards to both but the cowboy drew defeat.

Harry Knight came out to lend a hand and the boys all gathered round,
But Pete cashed in before they took him through the gates of the infield ground.

Every word I've said is true, boy's I tell you so,
T'was in Harry Rowell's arena on that Sunday long ago.

A quiet country graveyard, just outside of town
"The Lone Tree Cemetery" is where they laid him down.

Up there in the Cowboy Hall of Fame, I am sure the Lord would write,
World Champion Bronc Rider, beside the name "Pete Knight".

John D. McCulloch

"RODEO HALL OF FAME SERIES"

only was he a bronc rider but also a genuine horseman as well. He developed his own riding ability early in the 'Twenties at the small, one-day cowboy celebrations in the vicinity. I saw him make an outstanding ride at one of these shows where he won first prize.

Pete Knight, the greatest bronc rider of his time.
Linder Collection

"I asked him to attend the Stampede that I was producing at that time in Calgary. From then on, he started to take them all in, and with the passing years, he has appeared in about every contest in both the United States and Canada, as well as Mexico, England and Australia.

"His success is well-known. As a rider of bucking horses, he was acknowledged tops everywhere he went. Success never changed him. He was always the same, unassuming boy that he had been when I first saw him ride at that little, one-day show when he won his first prize. Despite the fact that his father bought land in Alberta, and his brothers farm here, too, Pete was not a Canadian. Neither was his home Calgary, as he was often billed. He was born in Philadelphia, Pennsylvania, May 5, 1903, His family moved to Stroud, Oklahoma when he was a small boy. Then they moved to Alberta, and Crossfield was their nearest town. Although he owned land near Crossfield, he gave his address as Denver, Colorado until the arrival of his daughter, Deanna. Then he decided to make his permanent home in California.

"His wife, Ida Lee, was known to thousands of his rodeo friends as Babe. She has the sincere sympathy of all who knew Pete. He was a top bronc rider, a fine fellow, a real man, and a devoted husband ..."

Herman Linder is another to share his thoughts regarding the Crossfield cowboy. Herman appeared at many rodeos with Pete from 1929 to 1937 and the two were both involved in the Boston Garden Strike in 1936 being original Turtles.

Although the two never travelled together, Herman recalls an evening spent with Pete and wife Babe in Deadwood, South Dakota. Herman also remembers the rodeo in New York's Madison Square Garden in 1935 when Pete finished first in the saddle bronc event and Herman came second. Pete won a saddle and a pair of chaps, as well as prize money.

"Go ahead and take the chaps, you earned 'em," said Pete. And they became a valued souvenir of his rodeo days when Herman ended active competition in 1939. Today, the chaps can be found in a cowboy museum in Lewiston, Idaho.

"I was in Fort Worth, Texas with Pete two months before he was killed. He was heading for California, and asked me if I was coming along. I told him I had crops to put in and cattle and calves to look after back home and that I'd be seeing him later on in the summer, which of course, I never did. We shook hands and said goodbye there at the hotel. He was

Pete Knight is seen, far right, in 1923 with Eddie, far left, and May Watrin, second from right, and Elyene and Pat Smith.
Linder Collection

105

Pete Knight winning 1930 World's Championship at Cheyenne, Wyoming.
Photo Linder Collection

Pete Knight's last ride on the bronc Duster, May 23, 1937.
Photo Rowell Rodeo History Book

one of the greatest, if not the greatest bronc rider that ever lived. Pete's death was a big blow to all of us."

Echoing Herman's sentiments about Pete was Willard Porter who wrote the following in 1984 in *The Sunday Oklahoman* under the title, Bronco Riding: Spill Killed Rodeo's Shining Knight:

"Pete Knight's career had colour, drama and tragedy. In addition, his skill in the saddle on the back of a bucking horse was a beautiful sight to behold.

"At maturity, Knight was a powerful man, a rider who used his ample strength to combat the antics of the wild, determined rodeo horse. But he also had the balance of a Herman Linder, a Jerry Ambler, or a Casey Tibbs, splendid, yet much lighter rodeo riders. He combined, in graceful fashion, his power and his balance.

"It was the exceptional horse that was able to unseat him.

"In the 1920s, he limited his activity to Canadian rodeos, sticking close to the little Alberta ranch he had purchased, partially from rodeo winnings. He owned bucking horses himself, contracted them to rodeos and practiced on them when he could.

"At Calgary in 1927, fans saw him win both the North American and the Canadian Bronc Riding Championships, a feat he repeated six years later.

"Starting in 1930, he began touring the United States rodeo circuit and it didn't take long to tame the roughest horses and impress the toughest hands. From 1932 through '36, he won the World Saddle Bronc Riding Championships four times, giving it up to Leonard Ward of Talent, Oregon in 1934.

"He was on his way to a fifth championship in 1937 when he drew Duster at Harry Rowell's Ranch Rodeo at Hayward.

"It has been said by men in the know that Knight, through the years, drew Duster — and rode him — eight times. So as he settled down on the Rowell-owned brown gelding that day, nobody expected anything extraordinary to occur.

"Many cowboys have tried to figure out what did happen, because what did happen, according to fair and honest rules, should not have happened.

"Pete was bucked over the horse's head and Duster could not avoid stepping on him. The cowboy was killed — in the prime of his career.

"Though he was able to get up and walk, assisted, from the arena, he died on the way to the hospital when a broken rib punctured his spleen."

Asked writer Porter:

"How and why did it happen? Fatalists still say it was just one of those things that happen that need no reason. It was simply fate.

"More realistically, others say something did happen. Johnnie Schneider, a twister who was helping Knight saddle up, is one of these. He remembers seeing Duster hit the side of the chute as horse and rider moved into the arena. He thinks the blow knocked both horse and rider out of balance.

"Bronc riders accept this explanation. They liked and admired Pete Knight. They want a good, solid reason for his death when they look back on it, as they often do.

"The fate thing just won't work with them," concluded Porter.

Rodeo producer Harry Rowell paid for the funeral, and for Pete's burial at Lone Tree Cemetery in Hayward.

Another Look At Pete's Death

Pete Knight of Crossfield, Alberta was one of the great names in saddle bronc competitions.

Pete was cut off in his prime during a rodeo in California. His death proves that rodeo riding is a sport more dangerous than average.

Pete Knight took his last ride on May 23, 1937.

It was the 18th annual rodeo at Hayward, California, a contest sponsored by Harry Rowell, a small contest, but not at all strange to rodeo, and one that drew some of North America's top hands.

Doff Abert had just been bucked off and was making his way across the arena when the announcer's voice boomed out:

In Memory Of

Our Friend, Pete Knight

Our memory of "THE" staunch cowboy
Is a friendly smile and a word of joy,
To all cowboys from either land
Willing to help, was this great hand.

As a champion, he was unsurpassed,
During the years his riding did last;
None were too large; none too small
With his nerve of steel he'd challenge all.

From earthly cares he is now redeemed;
Cruel to his friends it may have seemed.
But his Maker surely knew what was best,
When He took our dear friend away to rest.

He is gone Beyond — where good cowboys go;
When we shall meet him, we do not know.
So let our memories be what they shall,
Good they must be — who knew him well.

A tribute by Agnes and Herman Linder, 1937

Pete Knight is shown "lying in state" prior to his funeral at Hayward, California following his tragic death May 23, 1937. He was buried in the Hayward Lone Tree Cemetery. The picture at right shows Pete's casketed remains being re-interred at the Greenwood Cemetery, Hot Springs, Arkansas, Feb. 8, 1960, on the instructions of his widow, Ida Lee (Babe) Knight.

"Out of Chute No. 3, Pete Knight riding Duster!"

Duster was considered one of the roughest broncs in bucking contests at that time. But Pete, who had bested Duster several times before, was still in the saddle at the end of eight seconds.

Just before the ten-second signal, Duster stumbled, then trampled Pete while the two were lost in a cloud of dust.

Harry Knight, no relative, but a close friend of Pete, reached him first. "Are you hurt, Pete?"

"You're gawdamned right I'm hurt!"

Pete got up, waved aside a stretcher, and limped from the arena. It was a characteristic gesture and a fatal one. In walking unassisted from the arena, Pete rammed a broken rib into a vital spot. He died on the way to the hospital.

His friends buried him in one of those inexpressibly lonely California graveyards, not far from the arena in which he made his last ride.

Later, much later, his body would be exhumed at his widow's request, and re-interred in Greenwood Cemetery, Hot Springs, Arkansas February 8, 1960.

Bucking Broncs And Broken Bones

"...Discharged from Lethbridge hospital today after spending fifteen days for operation on my left leg which was injured in a rodeo many years ago."

- Linder diary Oct. 15, 1990

Herman Linder was eighty-three years of age when he left hospital with a knee that was "practically new" after suffering pain and discomfort for a number of years.

Broken bones and bruises are part and parcel of the cowboy's lot and working on a ranch can also bring its aches and pains.

Here's how this lithe and nimble individual fared over the years:

July 27, 1932	"The last day of the Lethbridge Stampede. A steer jumped on my back and crippled me up a little."
Sept. 3, 1933	"Bucked off in the Saddle bronc riding at Chicago. Hurt my back. Stopped at drug store and got some dope to rub on the sore spots."
Oct. 12, 1933	"Horse reared in chute and skinned my leg up."
Jan. 15, 1934	"Neighbour Zemp at Cardston asked me to help saw some wood. Got my left hand in the saw. Sewed up my fingers in hospital and told me I'd be here a few days. Worried about my riding hand."
June 20, 1934	"Fell heavily while getting off my saddle bronc in London, England. Sprained ankle, leg swollen up."
July 9, 1934	My decorating steer at Calgary Stampede ran into the fence with me and almost killed the cameraman."
Oct. 20, 1934	"We had three shows at Madison Square Garden in New York today. I rode *Old Man Of The Mountain* and he fell on my leg and hurt it quite bad."
Nov. 11, 1935	"*Big Boy* bucked me off at Boston Garden rodeo. Stepped all over me. Broke some ribs and put me in hospital."
June 13, 1936	"Steer hit me in the head with a horn while riding at Visalia, California."
July 11, 1936	"I got kicked in the face by a bronc at the Calgary Stampede. Still won four titles and brother Warner, though badly crippled up, won calf roping and steer decorating events."
July 14, 1936	"Won first day money in the steer riding at Yorkton, Saskatchewan rodeo but also sprained my ankle and will have to sit out the rest of the show. Sure feel bad."
July 5, 1937	"The big show at Calgary got off to a good start. Injured my knee the first event I worked. Am out for the week."
Sept. 28, 1937	Bucked off my horse and steer at Oklahoma City. Hurt my wrist bad."
Dec. 16, 1937	"A crew of seven helped finish shingling our barn. I got a terrible itch in the evening and later had bumps all over my body. Hands swollen bad."
March 24, 1938	"Have spent eight days here in Australian hospital after my horse fell while roping a steer. Lips swollen, eyes swelled shut. Terrible sore."
May 29, 1938	"Horse reared in the chute at Chicago. Messed me all up. Sure felt bad."
June 30, 1938	"Got jammed in the steer decorating at Claresholm, Alberta yesterday. Home all day. Passing a lot of blood."
April 26, 1939	"Have been feeling rough. Discovered I have Chicken Pox. ."
Aug. 17, 1939	"Turned the rest of my stock out after *Bell Boy* fell with me and hurt my back at Sidney, Iowa show. I felt blue so Leo Murray and I decided to get tight. We did."

Herman walks through the snow to the ranch house, his step "less spritely than then."

HG Photo

March 9, 1957	"Discharged from Cardston hospital after five days for hernia operation."
Aug. 24, 1965	"Spent more than a month in hospital in Cardston and Calgary. Operation on back for bone chip pressing on a nerve."
Aug. 17, 1965	"All well until 5:30 p.m. when Tom jerked tractor on me as I was trying to do up hitch. Agnes took me to hospital. Have broken pelvis."
Aug. 28, 1965	"They wheeled me down elevator and I saw daughter Rosemarie married to Tommy Bews. They then left for Lethbridge for church wedding and reception.
Sept. 13, 1965	"Agnes brought me home from hospital. I have spent nearly one hundred days on my back."
July 8, 1966	"Got horses in and grey mare kicked me. Had an evening rodeo at Fort Macleod. Smashed my fingers loading Fox."
July 8, 1967	"Rodeo went well at Fort Macleod until a riderless bareback bronc broadsided my horse while I was arena director."
Aug. 3, 1967	"Healing well from eight broken ribs and a punctured lung. Agnes and daughter-in-law Kia came to take me home."
June 25, 1978	"Was milking cow 311 when she kicked our calving door and hit my head, splitting my right ear. Went to the hospital and got it sewed up."
July 6, 1983	"In hospital after my horse bucked me off at the ranch and broke my nose. They put me to sleep and straightened it out."
Aug. 17, 1983	"Went by horseback to move bull over to the coulee. The bull bumped my horse so hard we both fell and I got a broken hip. My horse headed back home and the family came looking for me. I laid in the pasture for an hour."
Aug. 26, 1983	"Going home on crutches after getting a plastic ball in my hip in Lethbridge hospital."
July 8, 1994	"Rode in the Calgary Stampede parade as part of rodeo committee. Afterwards, Ed Rutherford and Mark Roy tried to hold my horse for me to dismount. Somehow things didn't work out good. Had a wreck as I fell and my horse hit me in the head. Had to go to first aid room to stop the bleeding."

The Greatest Outdoor Show On Earth

"... I got kicked by a horse and was in bad shape at Calgary, but finished first in bareback, first in bull riding, second in the Canadian saddle bronc riding and third in the North American saddle bronc. Also won the Calgary Stampede All-Around Cowboy Championship for Canada and North America. The announcer jokingly asked the people to kindly leave so I could take the grandstand home with me, as well. Brother Warner also won the calf roping. Sure was happy."

—Linder Diary, July 11, 1936

The Calgary Exhibition and Stampede Had Its Start Early In The Century

The seed that was to grow into the world renowned Calgary Exhibition and Stampede was planted in the fertile soil at the confluence of the Bow and Elbow Rivers in 1884. It was then that the editor of The Calgary Weekly Herald observed that an agricultural "fair" should be encouraged in order that agricultural products could be collected and displayed for the community of twenty-five hundred.

These observations led to the formation of an Agricultural Society on August 16, 1884. For a basic fee of one dollar, interested individuals could become involved in the district's agricultural advertising and promotion. Proposals were formulated, and the fair was planned.

History intervened, however, with the staging of that first show. The Riel Rebellion swept across the Prairies in 1885, and a concerned community watched as Louis Riel and his Metis friends fought for the rights of their people.

With peace restored, the Society reorganized in 1886, with Colonel James Walker, ex-Royal North West Mounted Police, elected as the first president. Under his leadership, Calgary held its first Agricultural Fair on October 9, 1886. Prize monies in the neighbourhood of $900 were offered, and the fair drew a crowd of about five hundred.

With such a roaring success to their credit, the Society made the fair an annual event.

Young Herman when he attended his first Calgary Stampede in 1929.　　　*Linder Collection*

Calgary Stampede poster for 1912.
Glenbow Archives NA-1216-1

sustaining, and the grounds became city property when the city paid the fair's $7,000 deficit in 1900.

It was the turn of the century, though, and with the hope of a new era to spur them on, the Calgary Agricultural Society reorganized as a no-dividend, joint stock company under the name of the Inter-Western Pacific Exposition Co. Ltd. The organization enjoyed modest prosperity, and in 1908 hosted the Dominion Exhibition, elevating it to the status of a significant national event. In 1910, the company again changed its name, and the Calgary Industrial Exhibition Co. Ltd. was born.

The stage was now set, and in 1912, Guy Weadick, a trick roper who had played more than his fair share of Wild West shows, vaudeville and travelling rodeos, arrived in Calgary. Weadick (for whom a Calgary public school is now named), was ready to take centre stage, and he saw Calgary as the crossroads of the Canadian West. He envisioned it as the birthplace of the biggest "frontier days show the world has ever seen ... hundreds of cowboys and cowgirls, thousands of Indians. We'll have Mexican ropers and riders ... we'll make Buffalo Bill's Wild West Extravaganza look like a side show..."

Weadick was a dreamer, but a dreamer with a difference. As well as being a showman and a performer, Weadick was a promoter and organizer,

Stampede founder Guy Weadick and wife Flores La Due at their Southern Alberta ranch.
Linder Collection

In July of 1889, ninety-four acres of the land which would eventually comprise Stampede Park were purchased from the Dominion Government. Canada's economy during that time was less than stable and the newborn society fell on hard times. So desperate were their financial straits that, on occasion, directors had to sign personal notes to keep the fair running. City Council, realizing the contribution that the Fair Society was making to the quality of life of the frontier town, occasionally provided grants to offset the general expenses of the fair. However, it finally became obvious that the agricultural showcase of the community could not be self

A.E. Cross

George Lane

A.J. MacLean

Patrick Burns

The Big Four bankrolled the first Calgary Stampede.

and he had the substance to make his dream a reality. The only thing this cowboy lacked was money.

He haunted the lobby and the bar of the Alberta Hotel and told his story to anyone who would stop and listen. Finally, a meeting was arranged with E.L. Richardson, General Manager of the Calgary Industrial Exhibition. Faced with an exhibition that had been slowly losing steam and needing a new spark of life, Richardson was intrigued and thought that Weadick's "hair brain scheme" might keep the exhibition from sinking into the red again. But, when Weadick talked about a $100,000 bankroll, Richardson backed away. He assured Weadick that if responsible financial backers came along, he was prepared to recommend a rental of the Exhibition grounds, but beyond that, he could not afford to get involved.

As Weadick, frustrated and dispirited, returned to the Alberta Hotel, he was met by a man who had heard his story., He introduced himself as H.C. McMullen,

Maurice E. Hartnett
... longtime General Manager
of the Calgary Stampede

general livestock agent for the Canadian Pacific Railway. He listened to Weadick's proposition and asked for a week to arrange a meeting between Weadick and four prominent Calgary ranchers: George Lane, A.E. Cross, A.J. MacLean and Patrick Burns. These men, later known as "The Big Four", agreed to back the project to a total of $100,000 and the deal was cemented with a handshake. It would be known as "The Stampede" and if it proved to be as successful as Weadick expected it to be, the word "Stampede" would always be synonymous with Calgary.

Thus, the stage was set and the script written for "The Greatest Outdoor Show On Earth."

The first Stampede, (four days then and ten now) held in September of 1912, was everything Weadick promised — and a resounding public success. The opening performances were attended by more than fourteen thousand enthusiastic Calgarians and visitors.

The city of forty-seven thousand welcomed the Duke and Duchess of Connaught and their beautiful daughter, Lady Patricia, to the Stampede, and the Duke, a son of Queen Victoria and Governor-General of Canada, opened the show.

There was a Stampede parade down Stephen (Eighth) Avenue, featuring a mounted cowboy band from Pendleton, Oregon, hundreds of cowboys, cowgirls and Indians, and City Hall was decorated with twenty thousand electric lights.

There was much to celebrate as Tom Three Persons, a Blood Indian from Cardston, Alberta rode the outlaw horse Cyclone to a standstill and won the World's Bucking Horse Riding Championship. He received $1,000 in cash, a handmade saddle and a championship gold belt buckle.

Clem Gardner of Pirmez Creek, a district west of Calgary, was another Canadian winner, claiming the title of Canadian Champion All-Round Cowboy. The Canadian bronc riding title went to Thomas Gibson of Calgary with "Red" Parker of High River, second.

Fred Kennedy would explain in his history of the Calgary Stampede that there were few front delivery and no side delivery chutes in those days. The bucking horses were led into the centrefield blindfolded and saddled; the contestant was then allowed to mount and set himself firmly in the saddle before one of the team snatched off the blindfold, while the other man turned loose the halter rein. There was no eight second ride; a

Four Albertans with a lot of background in rodeo include, from left: Lorne Thompson, Medicine Hat; George Edworthy, Calgary; Dick Cosgrave, Rosebud and Herman Linder Cardston.   *Linder Collection*

cowboy was required to ride his horse full out. When the judges figured that he had conquered his mount they would blow the whistle to signal the end of the ride.

In that first 1912 Stampede, three Alberta cowboys swept the boards in the cowboys' one and one-half mile relay race which was one of the feature events of that first show.

The best time of the week was turned in by Jimmy Mitchell of Medicine Hat, Alberta, who won $750, "Dug" Wilson of Claresholm placed second and won $500 and Harry Bray of Medicine Hat received $300 for placing third.

Another winner was Flores La Due, who in private life was Mrs. Guy Weadick. She scored a narrow victory in the cowgirls' fancy roping event.

Patrons of the first Calgary Stampede saw steer bull-dogging for the first time. This was an event which saw a cowboy jump from the back of a galloping horse onto the horns of a running steer, stop him and then wrestle him to the ground.

Financially, the Stampede did well. Revenue was $123,000 and expenditures $103,000. But some earlier commitments would detract from a somewhat rosy financial picture.

THE CALGARY STAMPEDE SOME YEARS LATER

"...Cowboys don't get to do this sort of thing. Usually its a King or a Queen or a Governor-General or famous soldier or politician. For the Stampede to ask me to officially open the show — it's like a dream."

Linder Diary, July 9, 1982

The First World War called the cowboy to battle and delayed a second Stampede until 1919 — although Weadick put on another show in Winnipeg in 1913.

With the signing of the Armistice on November 11, 1918, Weadick decided to make one more attempt to interest the Big Four in staging what he called a "Victory Stampede."

In the spring of 1919 Weadick returned to his adopted city with high hopes for a second Stampede, and immediately approached the same four men who backed the show in 1912. They were interested ... on the following

Eddie Watrin on Black Nitre *at the 1933 Calgary Stampede.*
Linder Collection

and thrilling to give this Stampede something extra to catch a visitor's eye. He settled on Chuckwagon racing and thus, the Rangeland Derby was born in 1923.

There are many different stories as to how the Chuckwagon races began. Some old timers say Weadick got the idea from wagon races cowboys held on the open range. Others say the idea came from a practice during land rushes when settlers in wagons raced to reach a certain piece of property they wanted to claim. Some say the "chucks" revolved around some Round-Up crews racing their chuckwagon and riders for the last half mile which separated the outfits from the nearest town and saloon at the conclusion of the Round-Up. The last crew in usually stood the winners one round of drinks.

terms: if thirty Calgarians could be found who were willing to gamble $1,000 each for a total of $30,000, the Big Four would guarantee to match that amount. This was accomplished with very little difficulty and the "Victory Stampede" took place.

Under Weadick's guidance, the second colourful show was a tremendous success and resulted in a small profit, which would be evenly divided between the Great War Veterans Association and the Young Men's Christian Association.

With the enthusiastic support of local citizens and the distribution of profits to worthy organizations, the Stampede had earned the ongoing support of Calgarians on a year-to-year basis.

In 1922 the Stampede was still a separate entity from the Calgary Exhibition and Richardson, still general manager, was worried about the financial condition of the Exhibition. Finances were dwindling and, at the annual meeting of the board in 1922, he recommended an experiment with the Stampede as an attraction — on a one-year trial basis.

Weadick was elated and worked with a will to find something new

Guy Weadick at Calgary. Behind him is Tom Three Persons.
Glenbow Archives NA-161-3

Top hands at the 1938 Calgary Stampede, from left: Jack Dillon, Herman Linder, Sykes Robinson, Jack Wade, Cecil Bedford, Charlie Ivins and Dick Cosgrave.
Calgary Photo Supply Co.

In twelve years of driving his own rig from 1926 to 1943, Dick Cosgrave of Rosebud, Alberta won the Chuckwagon title ten times — another Calgary record that has never been equalled.

In 1923, after a successful courtship, the Calgary Exhibition and Stampede became one and the same, It would be a winning combination of great rodeo excitement, agricultural initiative, and the first chuckwagon races under competitive rules. Patrons would see The Prince of Wales (later the abdicating Edward VIII) present the silver trophy to Canadian Bronc Riding Champion Pete Vandermeer.

"...Here at Calgary in the Grand Finals I won first in Canadian saddle, bareback and steer riding. Also second in the open saddle bronc contest. Also won all-around cowboy championships for North America and Canada. My honey and I are sure happy. At the night show I got nine trophies. We had special seats. The fireworks are grand."
—*Linder Diary, July 14, 1934*

In 1952, Guy Weadick was an honoured guest at the Stampede, where he presented championship trophies to the victorious cowboys — forty years after he had organized that first Stampede. It was not only a fitting tribute to this visionary cowboy, but a timely one as well. Weadick's death — and subsequent burial at High River, Alberta December 21, 1953 — saddened many people — and he was laid to rest under the rolling foothills of the country he loved.

Today, in his honour, the Stampede offers the Guy Weadick Memorial Award, presented to the contestant who best combines outstanding accomplishments in rodeo with personality, sportsmanship and appearance. The trophy by artist Gina Cohoe of Cremona, Alberta shows a mounted cowboy trailing a steer. The award began in 1981 and starting in 1995, runners up received a bronze trophy by Rocky Barstad of High River. Trophy donors are J & L Supply Ltd.

"....The Big Show got off to a good start and I injured my knee the first event I worked. Am out for the week."
—*Linder Diary, July 5, 1937*

The Calgary Exhibition and Stampede expanded from its traditional six-day show to a nine-day show in 1967. Attendance rose by approximately one hundred and forty-five thousand and since 1968, Stampede guests

Herman Linder calf roping at the 1937 Calgary Stampede.
Oliver photo

have had ten full days in which to let their hair down and enjoy the flavor of the old west.

The year 1978 brought major changes in rodeo format to the Stampede infield with individual challenges giving way to team competition. Three years later, the Calgary Stampede introduced a dual style of rodeo which combined both the team and the traditional events.

In 1982, "The Greatest Outdoor Show On Earth" became even greater. The Stampede introduced the Half Million Dollar Rodeo — the richest purse ever offered in the history of the sport. Hundreds of professional cowboys compete in elimination rounds, narrowing the field for the winner-take-all final day of rodeo. Over a quarter of a million dollars is paid out in this grand finale infield competition, with the winners taking home $50,000 from each major event.

"... I was taken down to the parade route where they had a horse ready for me to ride. Bob Young later drove my small group to Rotary House for lunch. I was a head table guest. Then to the afternoon Stampede and back to Rotary House for dinner. I was a guest at the evening grandstand show and opened the Stampede."

—Linder Diary July 9, 1982

Warner Linder winning the calf roping at the Calgary Stampede in 1936.
Calgary Photo Supply photo.

The well-known artist and sculptor, Earl W. Bascom (left) is seen with Herman at the 1938 Calgary Stampede. A cousin to western artists Charles M. Russell and Frederic S. Remington, Bascom started sculpting at the age of sixty-two. He was a rodeo cowboy from 1916 to 1940, competing in the three roughstock events of saddle bronc, bareback and bull riding as well as timed events of steer wrestling and steer decorating. Bascom died August 28, 1995 at the age of eighty-nine years and is survived by his wife Nadine, of fifty-six years and five children. One son, John A., resides in Victorville, California.
Linder Collection

Over the years, the Calgary Exhibition and Stampede has evolved in a style which makes it unique among fairs and entertainment organizations. It is a completely self-supporting organization and more than three hundred permanent staff complement the efforts of a volunteer structure in excess of fifteen hundred. This group's constant efforts are aimed at bringing the citizens of Calgary and Southern Alberta varied recreational and entertainment opportunities on a year 'round basis.

For ten days in July the staff group grows to eighteen hundred and the volunteer numbers swell as Calgary rolls back the clock and brings the dreams of Guy Weadick to life. Each and every worker, volunteer or staff member fully realize the important part they play in staging world calibre entertainment for more than one million paying guests.

"... Attended reception for Stampede announcer Warren Cooper's retirement. Party given by Calgary Stampede."
— *Linder Diary July 12, 1973*

The Calgary Exhibition and Stampede! More than just a fair or an exhibition, it is the complete coordination of people and the tradition of hospitality that sprung from the log cabins and soddies of Alberta's early days. It's flapjacks and street dances, chuckwagons and trick riders, mean broncs and friendly smiles; a city opening its arms wide to say to friend, neighbour and visitor alike, "Howdy folks, we're glad you're here."

First and foremost, though, it's the biggest "frontier days show the world has ever seen ... hundreds of cowboys, cowgirls and beautifully-costumed Indians.

Guy Weadick had his dreams, but unlike most dreamers, he was able to turn them into the real McCoy ... the reality of the world famous Calgary Exhibition and Stampede.

Western singer Wilf Carter made Alberta and the Calgary Stampede famous with such songs as Headin' for The Calgary Stampede, Swiss Moonlight Lullaby, My Beautiful Yo Ho Valley *and many others.*
Linder Collection

Former performers on the Southern Alberta Rodeo Circuit include, from left: arena director Herman Linder; Lynn Randall, Newhall, California; and Peggy and Joe Zoppe, Seagoville, Texas.
HG Photo

COWBOYS TURTLE ASSOCIATION

Turtle Members Faced Punishment For Competing At Calgary Stampede

"...Took a vote here at Cheyenne and I was upheld fifty-five to five in my actions at the Calgary Stampede."

—Linder diary, July 27, 1938

Herman couldn't believe his eyes!

There, hanging on the cowboy notice board at the 1938 Calgary Stampede was this warning: "Any member of the Cowboys' Turtle Association who participates in the Canadian saddle bronc riding or Canadian calf roping event is subject to a $500 fine or suspension or both. Signed, Everett Bowman, President, CTA."

This was all news to Herman who successfully chaired the first annual meeting of the Turtles March 11, 1937 at Fort Worth, Texas, and was elected first vice-president at that time. Bowman, of Hillside, Arizona, was elected president and although, by most accounts, a good leader, could be bombastic and less than diplomatic in his dealings.

The bylaws of the CTA gave the president unlimited powers. Article II said: "The president shall preside at all meetings of the association and of the board of directors, and enforce all laws and regulations of the association."

Bowman looked at Calgary and Rule II of the CTA: "No CTA member shall be allowed to compete at an amateur rodeo. An amateur rodeo is one which is advertised as such and held for the benefit of cowboys with limited rodeo experience, and in which they are protected by excluding any cowboys because of experience in other rodeos or in which handicaps are placed on any persons entering."

A goodly number of Canadian cowboys were asking Herman if they would be fined or banished from the CTA for competing in the two Calgary events, especially designed for Canadians.

Herman assured them there must be some mistake and encouraged them to sign up for the contests. Many would do so. Herman would take the Canadian saddle bronc, Brahma bull riding, and Canadian and North American All-Around championships that year and Hugh Connell of Stavely, Alberta, the calf roping title.

Bowman was outraged with Herman and the Canadian cowboys and

119

Stewart Dewar riding the bareback horse, Sky Blue at the Calgary Stampede.
Glenbow Archives NA-446-25

demanded a showdown vote at a meeting of the CTA in Cheyenne July 27, 1938.

"I guess I made a good speech, telling the boys our Calgary events were to determine the best Canadians in the field. It was a national event at a local rodeo and there was nothing amateur about it at all," said a modest Herman. Bowman had his say, but lost out on a vote of fifty-five to five. He was livid with the results and threatened to resign as president, but cooler heads urged him to stay on. He agreed.

A similar question had risen at the Reno, Nevada rodeo, slated for July 4, 1938. They had bronc riding and calf roping open to the world and also bronc riding and calf roping contests open only to bona fide residents of the State of Nevada. Bowman ruled in advance that two Nevada men, Cliff Gardner and Ray McGinnis, both of whom were Nevada residents could not compete in the Nevada events and thereafter compete in events in which Turtles competed. Otherwise, they would be fined and barred from competing in other rodeos where Turtles were competing.

On July 1, 1938 the management of the Reno Rodeo Association received the following telegram from Prescott, Arizona:

"As long as you have championship events in bronc riding and calf roping open to all with award of Rodeo Association of America points there is no objection or fine for Nevada members of Cowboys' Turtle Association to participate in Nevada state championship bronc riding and calf roping provided no RAA points are awarded in either state championship events. (signed) Cowboys' Turtle Association, Paul Carney, James Minotto, (directors), and twenty-eight members." President Bowman's name was strangely absent from the telegram.

Herman felt the matter was cleared when things were aired at Cheyenne. Although vice-president of the CTA, the verbal exchanges with Bowman had taken their toll. He would never seek elected office again in the organization to which he had helped give birth.

Herman riding at the Calgary Stampede.
Linder Collection

From One Champion To Another

A signal honour came Herman Linder's way July 11, 1964 when the board of directors of the Calgary Exhibition and Stampede chose him to present prizes to the new cowboy champions.

The Stampede said in an earlier news release that in ten years of rodeo competition that started in 1929 Linder won a total of twenty-two titles at Calgary in saddle bronc riding, bareback bronc riding, steer riding and calf roping.

The release noted that besides competing at Calgary, Linder also took part in rodeos in the United States, Australia and England. He won titles at New York's Madison Square Garden; Sidney, Iowa; Great Falls, Montana; Lewiston, Idaho; Woodward, Oklahoma; Cheyenne, Wyoming; Fort Worth, Texas; Tucson, Arizona; Seattle, Washington and twice "Down Under."

In 1936 he went to Australia to compete in rodeos and in 1938 he made a return trip, both times claiming International "buckjumping" (Australian for "saddle bronc") cups in the process. He was also marking high at a London, England rodeo in 1934 before badly spraining an ankle getting off a bareback horse, forcing him to catch the next ship home.

In selecting Linder to do the honours at the final night of the Stampede, general manager Maurice E. Hartnett said the Cardston rancher exemplified the performance, spirit and character of the rodeo cowboy at a high level.

"Herman's contribution to the development and progress of the big annual western event over a ten-year period of competition was unsurpassed," Hartnett added.

The Herman Linder Championship Record At The Calgary Stampede

(Twenty-two championships in all — a record that has never been equalled.)

1929
- BAREBACK BRONC RIDING
- CANADIAN SADDLE BRONC CHAMPION

1931
- CANADIAN ALL-AROUND CHAMPION

1932
- NORTH AMERICAN ALL-AROUND CHAMPION
- CANADIAN ALL-AROUND CHAMPION

1933
- CANADIAN ALL-AROUND CHAMPION

1934
- BAREBACK BRONC RIDING
- BRAHMA BULL RIDING
- CANADIAN SADDLE BRONC CHAMPION
- CANADIAN ALL-AROUND CHAMPION
- NORTH AMERICAN ALL-AROUND CHAMPION

1935
- BRAHMA BULL RIDING
- CANADIAN ALL-AROUND CHAMPION
- NORTH AMERICAN ALL-AROUND CHAMPION

1936
- BAREBACK BRONC RIDING
- BRAHMA BULL RIDING
- CANADIAN ALL-AROUND CHAMPION
- NORTH AMERICAN ALL-AROUND CHAMPION

1937
- INJURED IN THE FIRST EVENT

1938
- BRAHMA BULL RIDING
- CANADIAN SADDLE BRONC CHAMPION
- CANADIAN ALL-AROUND CHAMPION
- NORTH AMERICAN ALL-AROUND CHAMPION

Trophies and the Calgary Stampede

As a sporting contest the Calgary Stampede over the years has developed an imposing roster of athletic superstars.

Probably the most famous cowboy of them all was Pete Knight of Crossfield, Alberta who won the International Rodeo Association's World's Saddle Bronc Riding Championship four times and the Calgary Open Championship three times.

Everybody's choice for the All-time Canadian All-Around Cowboy would be Herman Linder of Cardston, Alberta who practically "owned" the Calgary Stampede from 1929 to 1939. He competed in: North American saddle bronc, Canadian saddle bronc, bareback, bullriding, calf roping and steer decorating competitions. He won twenty-two championships along the way — a record that has never been equalled.

Linder could win with a saddle or riding bareback. He won the bull riding. He came close to winning the steer decorating a number of times. He won the Canadian All-Around championship seven times, and the North American five times in a row.

Tops in chuckwagon was Dick Cosgrave of Rosebud, Alberta who won the championship ten times before retiring to become the arena director in 1949.

The star in calf roping was Pat Burton of Claresholm, Alberta who won eight roping championships between 1932 and 1940.

From A Brand Of Its Own — the 100 year history of the Calgary Exhibition and Stampede by James H. Gray, Western Producer Prairie Books, Saskatoon.

Newspaper Praises The Linder Brothers

Trumpeted *The Calgary Herald* in its Saturday, July 14, 1934 issue: "Turning in one of the greatest individual performances in the history of the Calgary Stampede, Herman Linder, youthful cowboy from Cardston (he was twenty-six at the time), won the Canadian bronc riding championship with saddle, the bareback bucking horse riding championship, the wild steer riding championship, came second in the North American bronc riding championship with saddle and was named both North American and Canadian all-around cowboy — the latter for the fourth consecutive year."

The Herald noted total attendance for the six-day show was expected to exceed two hundred and ten thousand.

Herman and brother Warner were featured in the Saturday, July 13, 1936 edition of *The Herald* as well.

"Linder Brothers Star in Stampede Finals" screamed the front page headline and roared again: "Herman Linder of Cardston, Kicked in Face by Wild Bronc, Best All-Round Cowpuncher".

Said *The Herald*: "Cardston cowboys wind up Calgary Stampede in blaze of glory with four firsts, one second and one third — Floyd Peters best North America calf roper — Thode wins bronc riding title — Harry Knight of Banff second to Arizona cowpuncher in North American final — Harley Walsh of Alberta again first in Canadian bronc riding championship.

"Staging the greatest two-man show in the history of the Calgary Stampede, Herman Linder and Warner Linder, brothers of Cardston, captured four firsts, one second and one third in the grand finals held at Victoria Park on Saturday afternoon."

According to *The Herald*, Herman Linder suffered painful injuries to the face when he was kicked by a bucking horse early in the afternoon of the rodeo finals.

"Linder fell when he jumped from Buckshot at the corral entrance on the east end of the arena, after completing his original ride in the Canadian bucking horse contest and was kicked in the face by his horse and knocked unconscious. He suffered a two inch cut on the side of the jaw and many smaller abrasions. Though stiff and sore and shaky he turned up for his remaining rides and finished them all with the crowd cheering his plucky action.

"The most sensational ride of the day was turned in by Linder when he drew Wildfire as a re-ride horse in the bareback bucking horse riding contest. Although still weak and dizzy, Linder stabbed the outlaw in the shoulder and then pawed him high in front and high behind until the whistle signalled the finish of the ride.

Sculptor Beil Was Protege
Of Western Artist Russell

Charles A. Beil was an eminent western artist whose work for the Calgary Exhibition and Stampede went back to 1934.

Beil began his art studies in Helena, Montana under the guidance of famous western painter and sculptor Charlie Russell, but his mastery of the sculptor's art was developed at his studio in Banff, Alberta.

Though his trophies for calf roping, steer decorating, bull riding and bronc riding were highly prized, some feel his finest piece was his bronze trophy for the chuckwagon races.

Beil put down his roots in Banff after the First World War. In 1934, he donated the C.A. Beil Trophy for the North American All- Around Cowboy and presented the bronze of a saddled horse to Herman Linder which can be seen at the Linder Ranch today.

Beil continued with his sculpting and, on pack trips into the Rockies, his path crossed that of G.H. Gaherty, president of Calgary Power (now TransAlta Utilities.) Beil was refining his skills as a sculptor and suggested to Gaherty that another piece of his work would make a suitable trophy for the Calgary Stampede. Gaherty agreed and Calgary Power supplied the trophy for the saddle bronc champion of 1939.

For thirty-two years, Beil did the Stampede up in bronze. When he eventually retired from the field in 1972, the Stampede board commissioned five other Alberta artists to supply the trophies. They were Gina McDougal, Malcolm Mackenzie, Douglas Stephens, Richard Roenish and Gerald Tailfeathers.

Another trophy treasured by Herman is the bronze of cowboy on a saddle bronc by Richard Roenish. It was presented when he officially opened the 1982 Calgary Exhibition and Stampede on July 8 of that year.

"Cowboys don't get to do this sort of thing. Usually it's a king or a queen or a governor-general or an outstanding politician. For the Stampede to ask me to do this sort of thing is just like a dream," Linder said.

Herman is seen in his den with his collection of rodeo memorabilia. The Calgary Stampede poster shown here used the picture of Herman riding Easy Money at the 1934 Stampede.
DS Photo

The Alberta Master Farm Family Award came to the Linder Ranch in 1971.

Calgary Herald Photo

1971 Was The Year

A Fitting Reward For The Linder Family

"...A great year for us. Good crops and good prices. Then to top it all off winning the Alberta Master Farm Family award was really something."

- Linder diary, December 31, 1971

There was great happiness in their home in September, 1971 when news arrived that the Herman Linder family of Cardston was one of five in Alberta to receive Master Farm Family Awards for 1971.

Although horses and rodeo had been constant companions for his sixty-four years, the award showed that Herman, with the help of his family, had paid close attention to crops, rangeland and cattle and was a contributing citizen to community and country.

The five families received a one thousand dollar cheque, a plaque and gate sign from the department of agriculture.

To be eligible for the award a family must have spent at least ten consecutive years in actual operation of a farm, be Canadian citizens and be nominated by at least three neighbours.

Nominees are considered first on a district basis, then at a regional level and finally by a provincial committee appointed by the minister of agriculture.

The awards are intended to honour Alberta farm families who have achieved notable success in farming, homemaking and citizenship, and to emphasize the advantages of farming as a life style.

Here's a picture of the Linder family, twenty-five years ago in 1971:

The Linders operate a sixteen hundred acre farm, six hundred of which are cultivated, with some four hundred acres in grain, fifty acres in hay and one hundred and fifty acres in partial fallow. The balance is rangeland for one hundred and twenty commercial cows. Sweet clover and cover crop are used extensively and for the past ten years, one hundred acres of the grain crop are put up as silage in a concrete pit silo. This is fed to all classes of cattle but mainly self-fed to approximately three hundred feeder cattle.

The Linders have an ability to link past experience with modern trends in farm and ranch management, something largely responsible for their success.

The family has taken part in a variety of community organizations and services, including the Western Stock Growers' Association, Cardston Agricultural Society, Unifarm, Telephone Board, Rural Electrification Association, Cardston Chamber of Commerce, Pacific Northwest Tourist Association, Rotary Club, Elks Club, Rodeo Historical Society of the U.S.A., director of the International Peace Park, Lethbridge and District Exhibition Association, Lutheran Church Ladies Aid and Mission League, Good Neighbours Club, Birthday Club and Women's Institute. Herman has played a key role in the development of rodeo as a professional sport in the 1930s, 1940s and 1950s. Agnes Linder is an efficient homemaker and keen gardener. She is active in the Southern Alberta Hereford Belles and the women's division of the Cardston Agricultural Society.

Many honours came to the Linders over the years. Herman was president of the Canadian Stampede Managers' Association for fifteen years and was made an honourary life president of that group. In recognition of his contributions to rodeo and rodeo management, Herman was made an honourary citizen of Fort Macleod, Alberta and Winnipeg, Manitoba, two communities where he staged rodeos for a number of years.

He is a member of the Kainai Chieftainship, official body of honourary

The Linder family in 1971, from left, George, Rosemarie, Herman and Agnes.

chiefs of the Blood Band. (Other noteworthy nominations and awards are found elsewhere in these pages.)

Herman and Agnes were selected to interpret the rodeo events at Calgary to Her Royal Highness Queen Elizabeth II, when she and Prince Philip visited Canada. The rodeo held during the Montreal (Quebec) Expo was arranged and managed by Herman in 1967. The 1971 amateur rodeo in Cardston was named "Linder Days" in his honour.

The Linders have two children — George and Rosemarie.

George, twenty-nine, and his wife Kia, have two daughters. They live in a modern home a short distance from the main residence. He earned a degree in agriculture from the University of Alberta and worked for two years after graduation with the Farm Credit Corporation before returning to the farm to take an active part in its operation. George is a member of the Range Management Society, a director of the Canadian Maine-Anjou Association, is active in 4-H and served on the executive of the Agriculture Club at the University of Alberta.

Rosemarie, twenty-seven, a registered nurse, married Canadian rodeo champion Tommy Bews of Pekisko, Alberta. They have two sons. She is a competent horsewoman, accomplished at barrel racing and steer hazing. Both George and Rosemarie have held executive positions in 4-H.

George looks after the books. Breeding stock is selected with the aid of Records of Performance (ROP) for rate of growth and gain ability. A crossbreeding program using artificial insemination introduced Maine-Anjou and Limousin blood to the herd. George does much of the AI and veterinary work himself.

Both generations exhibit a mutual understanding and respect for each other and a notable feature of this partnership is the respect Herman and George have for one another's contribution to the total operation. While Herman is open to the ideas his son has acquired concerning agricultural technology, George has a healthy regard for the wisdom, judgment and experience of his father.

The combined family efforts provide a practical example of farm and family progress and successful farm life.

"After lunch I typed out my reply speech. Got cleaned up. Ab Swinarton, Hughie Craig and Rider Davis came to congratulate us on our Master Farm Family Award. Dick Gray and party came then we all went to our big night. There was a large crowd there. We received many gifts. Was a great thrill to us."

- Linder diary December 3, 1971

It was a night to remember when two hundred and fifty people gathered in the Cardston Social Centre to pay tribute to the Herman Linder Family — one of five Master Farm Families in Alberta in 1971.

Nobody in attendance would know that two of the four Linders would be taken by death within the next fifteen years and the Linder & Son Ranch would later be sold to a young Mormon family, dashing the hope of a ranching dynasty.

But that was all in the future...

The Alberta Department of Agriculture put on a festive evening, assisted by the Cardston Rotary Club, the Municipal District of Cardston and the Alberta Wheat Pool.

Government awards and tributes were delivered following the banquet by Dr. E.W. Purnell, deputy minister of agriculture. Presentations were also made by Harold Jensen, Reeve of the M.D. and Bryce Cahoon, Rotary Club president.

Master of ceremonies for the evening was E.W. (Ted) Hinman, M.L.A. for the Cardston constituency and longtime friend of Herman. There were musical numbers and a comic reading.

Reminiscing by Herman, Agnes, Ted Hinman and others involved, along with the audience response, was indicative of the place the Linders held in the hearts and thoughts of neighbours and friends alike.

Herman has hosted people from around the world at the Linder Ranch. He is joined here by Mi Seong Kim of Pusan, South Korea who visited the ranch in 1994.
DS Photo

John Pratt, deputy director and producer of entertainment for Expo '67 reviews the Expo rodeo budget with Herman.　　*Linder Collection*

At right, The Rt. Hon. John Diefenbaker, former Prime Minister of Canada, speaks with Herman during a chance encounter in a western city.

Linder Collection

At right, Herman is seen in Mexico City in November, 1976 with incoming president Jose Lopez Portillo; Luis Echeverres Alvarz, president; and Jim Langley, Canadian Ambassador to Mexico.　　*Linder Collection.*

Camera Lens
Shows Herman's
Always On the Move

Cowboys young and old are seen at left. Herman has a kind word for buckaroos of all ages. He's with Matthew Synnott of Calgary, during a visit to the Stampede City.
HG Photo

At right. Herman joins Maine-Anjou breeder Wilma Flitton, seated, of Calgary and World of Beef editor Dorothea Schaab on the occasion of Wilma's birthday.
Linder Collection

Herman and the author, bottom left, attend a performance of "The Puff 'N Blow Boys" musical in Fort Macleod, Alberta. They're seen with cast members from the stage show honouring the memory of Alan Young. Program portions were also carried on CBC Radio.
Alberta Beef Photo

Attending the 25th anniversary sale at Perlich Bros. Auction Market, Ltd., Lethbridge are, from left: Valmer Bates, Cardston; Perry Yeast, Elkwater, Alberta; Ken and Tony Perlich, Lethbridge; and Herman.

128

At left, are Herman and Joy Young at the Linder Ranch. This book is dedicated to Joy's late husband, Alan. *Alberta Beef Photo*

The photo at right, was taken at the 1996 Cowboy Festival in Calgary and Herman, far right, accepted a plaque for friend Wilf Carter, presented by the Trail Riders of the Rockies. Jack McCulloch of Calgary holds a watercolour of Wilf Carter, while Clair Dezan, editor of the Wilf Carter News is at left. *HG Photo*

Below, enjoying 1987 brandings and rodeos in Alberta are, from left: Norm Edge, Cochrane; Alice Huggard, Stockmen's Memorial Foundation, Calgary; Herman, Cardston; Shirley Edge, Cochrane; and Gene Hanson, Airdrie.

Alberta Beef Photo

Herman and the late Hector McKay of Kathyrn, Alberta were great Maine-Anjou pals.
Alberta Beef Photo

A chilly day at the Linder Ranch

Photo by Bob Wotherspoon

Managing Stampedes Wasn't Easy While Herman Farmed and Ranched

Herman Linder was thirty-two and had been a pro rodeo competitor for ten years when he decided, in 1939, to give full attention to his ranching operation at Cardston and quit the arena of bucking broncs and mean-eyed bulls.

He did some judging at rodeos following retirement, and came into his own when he started producing rodeos in southern Alberta and British Columbia. He also staged rodeos at Edmonton, Alberta; Vancouver, British Columbia; Winnipeg, Manitoba and at the World's Fair (Expo) in Montreal, Quebec in 1967 ... the first rodeo to turn a profit at a World's Fair!

Here are some pages from his 1956 diary to show how ranching and rodeo were closely tied together. Herman was forty-nine years of age at the time:

May 15   Up at 5:30 a.m. and rolled up fence and cleaned up yard. Left at 10 a.m. for Calgary.

May 16   Arrived at Edmonton at 6:20 p.m.

May 17   Met Rex Allen at the plane. We got Buddy Heaton and Koko (Rex Allen's horse) on theatre stage. Was out to the grounds and arranged for the Stampede program.

May 18	Went over parade. Checked for Alberta Premier E.C. Manning to ride in parade. Very warm. Dinner at Hinman's.
May 19	Went to the grounds and checked things out. Was on TV.
May 20	Rex Allen, Slim Pickens and I went out to the girls riding club.
May 21	Parade at 11 a.m. and rodeo at 2 p.m. and 8 p.m. Crowds not too good. Feel very blue.
May 22	Rested all morning. We went to Kiwanis lunch. Very poor crowd again.
May 23	On TV again. Good rodeo and a little better crowd.
May 24	Had the best crowd yet tonight. Feel a little better. Judged gun-drawing contest in evening.
May 25	Rodeo again and Slim Pickens got kicked in the head. Almost a complete sellout for rodeo.
May 26	Had two performances. Very Warm. Had party in my room after show. Am happy rodeo is over.
May 27	Jack S. phoned me this a.m. that Henry Norris was killed on way home from our party last night. Had lunch with McKinnon's and went to Calgary. Feel blue over terrible accident.
May 28	Left Calgary early. Breakfast at High River and arrived Cardston at 2 p.m. Happy to be home. Yard progressing well.
May 29	Warner and I gathered the cows and put them in the home pasture. Hauled a load of hay to the bulls.
May 30	Branded our calves.
May 31	Louie, Warner and I cut my cattle and yearling heifers into Ellison field. Checked all cattle in afternoon.
June 1	Gathered our cattle at 5 a.m. and got cattle to Blackmore's by 5 p.m.
June 2	Moved cattle to Indian lease land. Lots of trouble running into cattle all along the way.
June 3	To Duce's this Sunday and helped brand after lunch.
June 4	Repaired broken fences.
June 5	Cut cattle from corral and took them to the Ellison.
June 6	To Lethbridge with Agnes for cattle sale.
June 8	Warner and I repaired fences on lease and ran out of posts. My back is still very sore.
June 9	Took bulls back over to the coulee. Cleaned out hopper and took mother to the drive-in.
June 10	Went to Monroe's to watch them rope. Hot. Bad dust storm.
June 11	Cold and windy, getting drier every day. Repaired fences on the lease.
June 12	Went across the line and helped open new tourist bureau. Came home and went to Chamber of Commerce meeting in evening.
June 13	Looked after business in town and signed contract for one hundred tons of hay.
June 14	Loaded Bill and went to the lease looking for horses. No luck.
June 15	Rained good last night. We are real happy.
June 16	Still raining. George and I went to Pincher Creek for horse sale. Checked with Royal Canadian Mounted Police regarding horses that are gone.
June 17	Went to Waterton Park for boat ride and picnic.
June 18	Warner and I went to town to investigate re black mare that has been stolen. We have been told who took her. Went to Glacier Park with the McKinnons for picnic.
June 19	Rode all day among the cattle on the lease.
June 20	Warner and I went to town to work on the rodeo grounds.
June 21	Rained quite hard last night. Found cow and calf of mine in river bottom.
June 22	Halter-broke the black mare that had been stolen. Went to Lethbridge to pick up the Australian boy (Rider Davis) at the bus station.

June 23	I went to the Lakes with Jack and Alister and rode in the parade. Had the boys meet the Boyles and Rider Davis. Went to Wilson's branding. Home at 9:30 p.m.
June 24	Did chores and wrote letters. Went over to Herb Christie's to watch the boys rope, then went to Bull Horn, where they were supposed to have horses in for Al and Jack to ride.
June 25	Put my bulls with the cows. Agnes and I went to the funeral for George Ross, Sr. of the Ross Ranches.
June 26	To Lethbridge for rodeo queen meeting.
June 27	Finished painting undercoat on new fence.
June 28	Repaired telephone line. Post broke and I fell to the ground. Took the Australian boys to the Indian Stampede.
June 29	Went to Foremost Stampede. Home by 8 p.m.
June 30	Rained all day. Raymond and Claresholm rodeos were cancelled.
July 1	Rained off and on all day. We rode through our cattle.
July 2	Australian boys went to Claresholm rodeo and we went to Raymond rodeo. Checked the bucking horses. Had flat on way home.
July 3	Rained all last night and rained hard all day. I went to High River and made up the rodeo program for tomorrow.
July 4	Things are too wet to rodeo so its been postponed. I went home and ran into a heavy shower.
July 5	We went to High River and posted Cardston rodeo bills along the way. Reg Kesler and I made up the Coleman, B.C. rodeo program.
July 6	Parade at High River in a.m. Rodeo ran off real fine. Finished at 5 p.m. George and I went to Coleman and arrived at 1 a.m. Mounties stopped us along the way.
July 7	Had a long parade. Big crowd so didn't start the rodeo until 3 p.m. Lunch at the mayor's party at golf clubhouse. Beautiful day.
July 8	Left for home at 10 a.m. Packed for Calgary.
July 9	Left home at 5 a.m. and got to Calgary fine. I went to rodeo alone. Agnes and I were with the Gordon Westgates and Fritzie Hansons for dinner.
July 10-13	Agnes and I attended Calgary Stampede.
July 14	The children and I took cows and calves to Cardston fairgrounds. Cloudy and cool.
July 15	Busy getting the Cardston rodeo program ready for the printers. Worked until midnight to get the second day done also. Beautiful day but had a heavy shower in the evening.
July 16	Took three horses to town and Rosemarie, George and I rode in parade. Good crowd and good rodeo.
July 17	Another nice day and good rodeo but not too big a crowd. It rained at the night show.
July 18	Up at 4 a.m. Brought our cows home from town. I went to Medicine Hat and got program made up. Went to Dirk Scholten's.
July 19	Big parade this a.m. Beautiful day and rodeo went over wonderful. At Hop Yuill's for supper.
July 20	Warm day and rodeo went off fine. Slim Pickens and I went out to Gene Burton's and then to Lorne Tansley's home.
July 21	Real scorcher of a day. Fine rodeo. Scholten resigned as president of the Medicine Hat Exhibition and Stampede.
July 22	To Scholten's for breakfast and later went to Mac Higdon's. Then headed for home.
July 23	I rode through our cattle out south. Found fence down and repaired.
July 24	I shovelled wheat in the bin. John and I repaired fence all afternoon. Warner finished drilling our cover crop.
July 25	Hauled three loads of wheat, the last of our 1955 crop. Cold north wind came up.
July 26	We started mowing hay on the Jensen field. Rosemarie and I went to the Lethbridge rodeo. I started the chuckwagon races.
July 27	Our family went to the Lethbridge rodeo and night show.

Miss Rodeo Canada Contest Started in 1957

Former Miss Rodeo Canada queens are seen together at the Herman Linder ranch in 1996. Back row, from left: JoAnne Perlich, Lethbridge; Dixie Forsyth, Raymond, Alberta, and Mary Lynn Beazer, Cardston. Front: Connie Ivins, Cardston and host Linder.   *HG Photo*

Rodeo queens from another era came together in Cardston in March, 1996 to reminisce about their experiences and for a photo shoot for the book, *The Linder Legend*.

The former Canadian queens gathered at the Linder Ranch, six miles from town, and included Connie Ivins and Mary Lynn (Cook) Beazer both of Cardston, Dixie Forsyth, Raymond, Alberta and JoAnne (Sharples) Perlich of Lethbridge, Alberta.

It was the first time the four queens had been together and they recalled that it was Herman Linder and the Southern Alberta Rodeo Circuit (SARC) that gave them the opportunity to vie for the Miss Rodeo America title.

In the early 1950s, the International Rodeo Association named Bob Latta of Casper, Wyoming, John Moss of Los Angeles and Herman Linder to a planning committee to set rules for The Miss Rodeo America Pageant. A queen would add glamour and beauty to the sport of rodeo and pay tribute to the contributions made by ranch women.

Twelve young North American women competed for the title in 1955 and were judged on horsemanship, personality and appearance.

Linder got the Southern Alberta Rodeo Circuit to endorse a queen contest and Connie Ivins was the first Miss Rodeo Canada Queen. She represented Canada at Casper, Wyoming in 1955 and was runner-up to the Queen.

"We built lasting friendships and it was a once-in-a-lifetime experience," said Connie.

Mary Lynn Beazer was Miss Rodeo Canada in 1956 and competed at the Golden Spurs

Herman is with Jennifer Douglas, 1995 Rodeo America Queen. The picture was taken at Colorado Springs, Colorado.   *HG Photo*

These young ladies vied for Rodeo Queen of America honours at San Francisco in 1957. Dixie Forsyth was Canada's representative and is fourth from left in the front row.

Herman is seen in 1995 with Lisa Eastman, Calgary Stampede Princess; Allison Boswell, Stampede Queen; and Karina Tees, Stampede Princess.
HG Photo

Rodeo in Chicago. She still remembers her first airplane ride, entertainer Don McNeill of the Breakfast Show fame and how kind Gene Autry was to all the contestants. Mary Lynn was named Miss International Ranch Girl during the contest.

Dixie Forsyth was Canadian queen in 1957 and competed for the America title at the Cow Palace in San Francisco.

"It was the first time I was ever that far from home. I remember we were riding in the arena and I was third in line when the saddle started turning on the girl in the lead. Without thinking, I rode up beside her and put her on my horse. Maybe I should have applied for pick-up duties at the rodeo," Dixie says with a mischievous smile.

A native of Claresholm, Alberta, JoAnne Sharples was named Miss Rodeo Canada at the Cardston Stampede in 1958 and competed in Las Vegas for Miss Rodeo America.

"Dad insisted we all go so there were four girls, Mom and Dad in a brand new Chevrolet, just packed to the brim. There was a parade in downtown Las Vegas and actor Gary Cooper was one of three judges. It was a real thrill to be there."

JoAnne, the wife of well-known Alberta auctioneer Tony Perlich, would later compete in the Miss Canada contest in Central Canada that same year.

For his part, Linder said the queen contest gave additional sparkle to the sport of rodeo, and he was glad to have had a hand in its formation.

Canadian rodeo queens no longer participate in the Miss Rodeo America competition, but they do attend as goodwill ambassadors.

For the past twenty years, Miss Rodeo Canada has been named at the Canadian National Finals Rodeo in Edmonton in November, but it is the SARC that is credited with the program's start.

JoAnne (Sharples) Perlich was Miss Rodeo Canada in 1958 and later competed in the Miss Canada contest. With or without the hat, it's still JoAnne that you see in the picture.
Calgary Herald Photo

The Rules Of Rodeo Were Fashioned From Experience

Much like democracy, the sport of rodeo was not invented, but evolved. And is still evolving.

Fast-paced action, mean-eyed bulls, bucking horses, daredevil clowns, the speed of an animal and split-second timing all contribute to rodeo, one of North America's fastest growing sports.

But participating cowboys and cowgirls know the actions of both horse and/or rider are being carefully evaluated by the eyes of judges and the hands of the stopwatch.

Rodeo events are divided into two classes: roughstock and timed events. Roughstock events, as the name implies, involves getting aboard a "rough" head of livestock — either a horse or a bull — and making an eight second ride before hitting the ground. Judges mark a qualified ride on the rider's style and aggressiveness; as well as on the wildness of the animal and how difficult it is to ride.

Calf roping, steer wrestling and ladies' barrel racing (there's little team roping in Canada) are determined by the stopwatch and possible barrier infractions.

The barrier is a thin rope stretched across the front of the box, the cowboy's starting point, which allows the calf or steer a predetermined head start. Should the contestant leave the box early, he receives a ten second penalty, which usually puts him out of the money.

Barrel racers also fight the clock. They all run the same course and best time wins. They don't have to fight a barrier, but they are penalized for knocking over any one of three barrels.

The following is a description of each rodeo event:

Saddle Bronc Event

Style and grace best describe rodeo's premier event. And balance and coordination are assets the good bronc rider can't do without.

Bareback and bull riding may call for great feats of strength as a powerful grip clings to a surcingle with handle or loose rope for the bull.

Frank Duce of Cardston on a saddle bronc.

The saddle bronc rider has only a rein attached to a halter with which to secure himself in his seat; and a saddle which must conform to rigid specifications.

A rider is rewarded for keeping in time with a horse; synchronizing his spurring action with the bronc's movements.

To qualify, the rider must have his spurs over the break of the shoulders until the horse completes his first jump out of the chute. He will be disqualified for touching any part of the animal, or equipment, or himself, for losing a stirrup, or getting bucked off before the end of the eight-second ride. Early on, it was a ten-second ride and at the start, the cowboy had to ride his bronc to a standstill!

Each event requires a key component to achieve success and for saddle bronc competition, this means maintaining a good rhythm.

An ideal spurring motion begins with the cowboy's feet over the bronc's shoulders as the horse's front feet first hit the ground. As the bronc bucks, the rider draws his feet back to the "cantle," or back of the saddle, before he snaps his feet back to the horse's shoulders just before the animal's front feet hit the ground again.

The equipment required by the competitor includes his own association approved saddle, spurs with dull rowels (the revolving disk at the end of each spur), leather chaps and a braided rein. The length of rein is crucial as it can mean the difference between staying on the bronc for the full eight seconds, or being tossed. By carefully adjusting the grip, the cowboy can maintain his balance and hopefully prevent himself from being pulled out of the saddle and over the front end of the horse.

There was a time at rodeos like New York where cowboys had no choice regarding saddle or bareback rigging. If he drew chute five, he'd use the equipment supplied by the management. No if's, and's, but's or maybe's.

Bareback Riding

The bareback bronc ride can be the most strenuous of rodeo's three riding contests.

The regulation eight seconds of each bareback ride are probably the longest in a cowboy's life. He must sit on a seemingly loco horse while it charges, bounds and reels around the arena. All the rider may grasp is the handhold of a bareback rigging — comprised of a leather strap connected to a hand-hold resembling a suitcase handle. This, in turn, is fastened to a cinch which securely straps the gear around the horse. No stirrups or rein are used in this event.

To qualify, the rider must mark the horse out of the chute by keeping his spurs over the break of the shoulders until the first jump out of the chute is completed.

The bareback rider will be disqualified if he touches the animal or equipment with his free hand or if he is bucked off before the eight-second ride is completed.

No other event in professional rodeo is as physically demanding as bareback riding. Using only one hand, the cowboy must hold onto the

leather handhold of the rigging which is customized to snugly fit his grip. The cowboy tries to spur the horse on each jump, reaching as far forward as he can with his feet and then bringing his ankles up toward the rigging.

It's the cowboy's arm that takes all the stress as it absorbs most of the horse's bucking power. While his arm endures this incredible tension, the cowboy's hand must remain intact with the rigging's handhold for the full eight seconds.

Bull Riding

The big Brahma bulls are hell on hooves — the most dangerous animals in rodeo. Perhaps that's why bull riding is the embodiment of rodeo excitement.

A bull weighs ten times that of the cowboy and the rider is faced with the tough task of staying aboard for eight seconds, then of jumping free without being gored, dragged, hurled, whirled or crushed by nearly a ton of beef on the hoof. A bull's built-in fury and nasty habits (like goring fallen riders and charging the rodeo clowns) is reason for an infield to be cleared in seconds.

The Brahma bull is a cross between the Brahma of India and the Mexican Longhorn, and is so easily agitated, that injuries sometimes occur before the chute gate is opened.

The bull rider is not required to spur his mount but will receive a higher mark if he does. A rider will be disqualified for hitting the ground before the regulation eight seconds expire or for touching the bull, or himself, with his free hand. A weighted bell, attached to a rope beneath

the bull, forces the rope to fall free when the ride ends — one way or the other.

Bull riding requires exceptional balance, and upper body strength and strong legs. Once again, the animal is marked on how difficult it is to ride. A crazily-spinning bull is considered the most difficult and, at the same time, it might leave the rider dizzy and helpless on the hard dirt of the arena. Pick-up men on horses cannot save the dismounted cowboy in this event because an enraged bull will invariably charge a man on horseback.

The rodeo clown is the cowboy's safety man and has saved many fallen and dazed riders from death or serious injury by quickly and fearlessly distracting vengeance-seeking bulls.

Calf Roping

Man and horse become one in this timed event: a single working unit which takes us back to the closest associations between the early cowboy and his treasured horse — when man's best friend was his horse.

The calf must cross the scoreline before the rider breaks the chute barrier or a ten-second penalty is added to his score. After roping the calf, the cowboy runs down the rope and throws the animal by hand. More time is lost if the calf is already down when the roper reaches the animal because the calf must be standing up before the cowboy may throw it down. Any three legs of the calf must be tied with a piggin' string. The tie is observed by a field judge and must hold for six seconds or the roper is disqualified. The horse who works with a calf roper must be able to judge the speed of the calf, be able to stop on cue in a single stride, and then hold the rope taut when the roper runs to his calf. Good roping horses are not easy to find.

Steer Wrestling

Rodeo audiences like this timed event in which a man drops from a galloping horse into the horns of a steer who is going full tilt, stops the steer and throws it to the ground in a matter of seconds.

Briefly, the secret is this: the steer must be caught from a horse. As the cowboy catches up to the steer, he reaches with his right hand, scooping up the right horn, and as his horse speeds by the steer, the cowboy gets this horn snugly in the crook of his right elbow. At the same time, his left hand pushes down on the other horn while his horse veers off to the left. The cowboy's heels are dropped ahead, and at a forty-five degree angle to the path the steer is taking.

Digging in his heels, the cowboy is tipping the steer's head as much as he can and pulling it toward the centre of a left-hand turn. As the steer stops — his hindquarters having swung around — the cowboy's left hand reaches for the animal's upturned nose and, with this hold, he is able to throw the steer on its side.

If the steer gets loose the dogger (cowboy) may take no more than one step to catch him. The steer will be considered down only when it is lying flat on its side, with all four feet and its head straight.

The winning run takes perfect coordination. Besides the steer wrestler and his horse, there is a second man, the "hazer", who starts from the opposite side of the steer. His job is to keep the animal running straight, retrieve the dogger's horse, and prevent any accidents.

Ladies' Barrel Racing

Barrel racing is a precision event in which horse and rider compete against the electronic eye-timer. As with calf roping, barrel racing requires close cooperation and teamwork between horse and rider.

A prizewinning barrel horse and rider combination is indeed a thrill to watch. The ability to ride a barrel horse properly while racing at top speed and making one-hundred-and-eighty-degree or three-hundred-and-sixty-degree turns takes both practice and patience.

Rosemarie (Linder) Bews at the Medicine Hat Stampede.

Herman is shown steer wrestling in Sydney, Australia in 1938. Clark Lund of Raymond, Alberta is the hazer. Horses in Australia were not neck rein broken at that time. Linder Collection

In the barrel racing competition, contestants circle three barrels in a cloverleaf pattern. The clock is stopped when the horse and rider have finished the cloverleaf pattern and crossed the start/finish line. A rider may touch or even tip a barrel; however, five seconds is added to total time if a barrel is knocked over.

Cowgirls have competed at rodeos since the turn of the century, not only in barrel racing, but in bronc riding, trick riding and calf roping.

Ladies' steer roping drew a lot of attention when introduced at the 1910 Cheyenne Frontier Days.

Fannie Sperry and Goldie St. Clair competed for the ladies' bronc riding title at Calgary in 1912. Florence (Flores) La Due left Coney Island, New York to do some fancy rope work in Calgary. Fox Hastings captured national headlines bulldogging at Houston, Texas, in the 1920s while Mabel Strickland made her appearance in steer roping at the same show.

My Very Best Wishes to "Agnes and Herman Linder" Alice Greenough

Herman remembers many female contestants at rodeos he attended in the 1920s and 1930s including Rose Davis from Texas, champion cowgirl of the New York Rodeo in Madison Square Garden; Alice Greenough, bronc rider and Tad Lucas, trick rider and bronc buster.

Barrel racing is said to have been born in 1945, when two Texas cowgirls, Jackie Worthington and Margaret Owens, suggested forming a group to be known as the Sponsor Girls who would conduct reining exhibitions and other demonstrations of horsemanship in the rodeo arena.

Herman's daughter, Rosemarie (Linder) Bews, participated in barrel racing for a number of years, and won at several rodeos.

And in 1996 it appeared ladies' barrel racing would become a "big ticket" item at the Calgary Stampede, offering a final $50,000 purse to the champions.

Boys' Steer Riding

Boys between ten and fourteen years of age generally compete in this sport, giving them their first taste of formal competition.

Native cattle are used, generally yearling or two-year-old steers. For spectators this can be a humorous part of the program.

The youngsters use the same kind of riding rope as the adult bull riders but may hold on with both hands. The ride is timed for eight seconds.

The young cowboy who can sit tight, do some spurring and, perhaps ride with one hand, and not two, will quickly get the judge's eye.

Today's boys' steer riding contestant is often your professional champion of tomorrow.

Wild Cow Milking

Wild cow milking originated on large cattle ranches. Cowboys rode through the herds checking for cows with calves which were not taking all the milk from their mothers. The cowboys then roped the cow and with one man holding the animal by the head, the other did the milking. Much easier said than done!

Each team must catch a wild cow, produce the required amount of milk in a pop bottle, and race to the judges' stand to record their time.

The milker has a helper (mugger), who is on foot and holds the cow's head; the roper milks the cow and it's up to the mugger to free the rope from the cow when the milking is done.

Wild Horse Race

A truly wild west event as teams of three cowboys: ear-man, shank-man and rider form a single unit to break a wild cayuse.

When the horses, wearing halters with long shanks, are released from the chutes, all three-man teams are hanging onto the halter shank. In each team, the closest man to the horse is the ear-man, followed by the shank, or anchor-man and then the rider who must also carry a saddle with him.

When the horn sounds, the team tries to bring the horse to a stop with the ear-man moving up the shank, grabbing the horse by the head. As the shank-man holds the horse, the rider quickly moves to saddle the animal, get on its back and ride it across a marked finish line.

This is a rugged and dangerous event and with several teams trying to saddle their horse at the same time, and in a confined arena, this amounts to chaos and mayhem.

Cutting Horse Contest

The skill of horse and rider is on view during a cutting horse event which is sometimes held in tandem with a rodeo.

Together, they can quickly separate a herd of cattle without the aid of pens and chutes. Here we see horse and rider work in harmony with a real western flavor.

The cattle used are generally yearlings, big enough to be handled and small enough to provide plenty of dust-raising action.

When the contestant is ready he is given the signal and then has less than three minutes to show the judges how well this man-horse team can work the cattle.

Horse and rider enter the herd, taking care not to upset the cattle. A particular animal is selected and quietly eased out of the group! Don't count on the critter staying away from the herd.

It's up to the mount and mounted to keep the animal singled out.

Points are lost if the cowboy quits a cow when not in complete control and if a contestant has to rein or spur his horse to maintain position. Point penalties are also imposed if the animal being worked gets past the contestant and returns to the herd.

The Rodeo Clown

That comical character who runs around the rodeo arena during the bull-riding events is not being paid to make the crowd laugh!

With the bulls as mean and dangerous as they appear, the rodeo clown is usually called on to endanger his life more than once during the rodeo. The clown uses his own body as a target to distract the bull from the cowboy who has finished his ride or has been thrown. Occasionally, a clown is called on to get in beside the crazed bull to free a cowboy's hand caught up in the bull-rope. The clown in the rodeo arena is being paid for a job similar to that of a lifeguard.

Rodeo clowns must be in peak physical condition because speed and agility are their main assets in their frequent confrontations with the bulls.

In many of the larger rodeos, the clowning is usually handled by two or three clowns and when there are several clowns one is usually a barrel-man. A barrel-man uses a padded barrel to dive into when the bull is in pursuit. The other clown or clowns will also use this barrel as a diversionary obstacle between them and the charging bull.

An enraged bull will often pitch the barrel all around the arena trying to get at the clowns while the barrel-man continues to cling desperately to the inside of the drum.

- Source: *Rodeo, A Spectator's Guide to the Sport of Rodeo*, Copyright Calgary Brewing and Malting Company Limited, June, 1971.

Slim Pickens was a great rodeo clown and was at his best when playing the role of bullfighter.
Linder Collection

Specialty Rodeo Acts

There is no such thing as slack time in rodeo. The action erupts all over the arena from the first event to the last and even when the stock is being loaded into the chutes or saddled, or the timed events are about to start, the show goes on.

One of the most popular "fillers" is the trick roper or rider.

One may see a dog act or specially-trained horses go through their paces. Clowns also have a special role to play when there is a break in the action or the infield may need watering down.

The Rangeland Derby

The Calgary Stampede claims the first chuckwagon race in world history, under competitive rules, in 1923.

According to Fred Kennedy in *Calgary Stampede*, about eight entries were received and the first rules went something like this:

1. Each chuckwagon outfit would have a regulation range food wagon, complete with chuck box, water barrel and camp stove;

2. The wagon would be drawn by four horses and each outfit would be entitled to four outriders;

3. There would be four teams to a heat;

4. The wagons would be required to line up in the centrefield in front of the chutes, and at a pistol shot, they would make a complete figure-eight around wooden barrels, head for the racetrack, run half a mile and then return to their original spot in the centrefield, unhitch the team, haul out the cook stove and the first team to "make smoke" would be adjudged the winner.

What the first race lacked in speed, it more than made up for in colour and excitement. Winner of that first Rangeland Derby was the team of Dan Riley (later Senator) of High River, Alberta. The top driver, with a record never to be equalled was Dick Cosgrave of Rosebud, Alberta. He won ten championships and claimed the Calgary Gas Company trophy outright.

Several changes have been made to the "chuck" races. Wagon canvasses are sold by public auction to support the rig owners and their outriders and horses. The safety of both men and horses has become a prime concern. Penalties are accorded for such things as knocking over a barrel, late or early outriders, rough driving and/or anything coming under what can be construed by judges as a race foul.

The Rodeo Stock

Herman Linder believes that today there aren't so many good bucking horses around, so the contractors try to save them and keep them bucking as long as possible. Horse power has given way to vehicle power and the horses no longer crowd the ranges.

"You can go to a rodeo show where there might not be more than nine or ten saddle broncs ridden, while it wasn't uncommon for us to have twenty-five to thirty saddle broncs ridden in one afternoon. I know when I rode in Lethbridge, Alberta and Cardston we rode at least fifty head of bucking horses, bareback and saddle broncs, in an afternoon."

Linder feels the best bucker is a combination between a draft horse and a thoroughbred, rather than the range bronc. That combination gives a horse more weight and adds more zip to the ride.

A change he applauds is that each rider now has his own saddle and the bareback contestants have their own special rigging. That wasn't so in the early days at many major rodeos.

Bucking horses, bulls, roping calves and dogging steers are the responsibility of the stock contractor.

In the early years of rodeo the stock used was wild and had to be brought in from ranches in the vicinity where the rodeo took place. Now, for the most part, stock used is owned by rodeo producers and taken from one rodeo to the next.

Contractors also employ extensive breeding programs and use good performing stock to produce more of the same.

The Calgary Stampede raises its bucking horses at the Calgary Stampede Ranch, 150 miles northeast of Calgary. Its home to three hundred and fifty head of bucking horses and covers twenty two thousand and five hundred acres.

The best of these horses will be away from home for thirty days, and they may be asked to buck fifteen times. That works out to one hundred and twenty seconds of labour or two minutes a year.

Generally, bucking horses are five years old before they get to show their stuff. A good bucking horse can be worth six thousand dollars or more.

National Finals Rodeo, North America's Largest

From The PRCA 1996 Media Guide

Cowboys work all year for a shot at the National Finals Rodeo, (NFR) the Professional Rodeo Cowboys Association premier championship event held each December in Las Vegas, Nevada.

The top fifteen regular-season finishers in each event qualify for the NFR and compete for prize money that will exceed $3.2 million in 1996.

Since its inception in 1959, the NFR has featured the top fifteen competitors in each of professional rodeo's seven events: saddle bronc riding, bull riding, bareback riding, calf roping, team roping, steer wrestling and barrel racing.

At the 1995 NFR, each of the ten rough stock, calf roping and steer wrestling rounds paid $33,440. Every round of team roping offered $41,800, and each barrel racing round paid $20,900.

The rough stock, calf roping and steer wrestling average payoff — the money reserved for the contestants who finish highest at the NFR — was $100,320 per event. The team roping average totalled $125,400 and the barrel racing average paid $62,700.

If a cowboy or cowgirl performs poorly at the NFR, it is unlikely he or she will capture a world title.

The PRCA did not always have a year-ending championship event. Before 1959, world championships were decided solely on the basis of regular-season earnings.

Dallas, Texas, was the site of the first NFR, which offered a purse of $50,000. After three years in Dallas, the fledgling event moved to Los Angeles, California.

After another three years, the NFR moved to Oklahoma City, Oklahoma, where it remained for twenty highly successful years. By 1984, the purse had climbed to $901,550.

In 1985, the NFR made another move, this time to its present home at Las Vegas' Thomas and Mack Center on the campus of the University of Nevada, Las Vegas.

Since then, the NFR purse has grown from $1.8 million in 1985 to more than $3 million in 1995. The Finals are contractually bound to stay in Las Vegas through the turn of the century, and the projected purse for the year 2000 is nearly $4 million.

The NFR is overseen by executive general manager Shawn Davis, a three-time world champion saddle bronc rider. He coordinates more than one thousand workers and hundreds of horse, bulls, steers, and calves.

About one hundred and seventy thousand people attended the sold-out NFR at Thomas and Mack last year, and an estimated viewing audience of thirteen million, three hundred thousand watched rodeo on ESPN and ESPN2.

Herman greets the crowd in Medicine Hat prior to that city's annual Stampede. That's Reg Kesler in the front seat.

Herman is seen with Doreen Kamis and former Member of the Legislative Assembly Gordon Shrake at a Robbie Burns night in Calgary.

Longtime friend Ward Robinson, right, welcomes Herman to the Simmental booth at the Calgary Stampede.

Wanderings with Herman

As a member of the Alberta Canada All Breeds Association (ACABA), Herman promoted and travelled on behalf of Alberta beef. ACABA directors in this picture included, front row, from left: Ken Copithorne, Calgary, Braunvieh; Norm Atkins, Leduc, Holstein; Dick Fisher, Longview, Limousin; and Tony Saretsky, Calgary, general manager. Back row, from left: Floyd Williams, Arrowwood, sheep and wool; Ward Robinson, Pine Lake, Simmental; Herman Linder, Cardston, Maine-Anjou; and Ken Lang, Olds, Charolais.
Alberta Beef Photo

Herman, centre, was named Male Athlete of the Century by the town of Cardston in 1987.
HG Photos

144

Leo Cremer was owner of the largest rodeo ranch in the world with over fifty thousand acres at Big Timber, Montana devoted to the care and raising of rodeo stock.

Doubleday Photo

Norman Haines, right, CEO, Western Heritage Centre, Cochrane, Alberta and wife Linda attend the unveiling of Robert Magee's painting of Herman on Easy Money.

The painting, "Winning It All" by Robert Magee forms a background for Herman and Adeline Linder, left, and Lydia and Brad Beazer of Cardston during the painting's unveiling in July, 1995.

Pete Armstrong, left, of Medicine Hat, Alberta welcomes Herman and Adeline to an auction on behalf of the Western Heritage Centre, Cochrane, Alberta.

Calgary Stampede is visitor time. Here, from left, we see Margaret and Paul Bond, of Nogales, Arizona; Adeline and Herman Linder; "Dutch" and Jerry Taylor, Graham, Texas; and Shirley Gunderson, Calgary.

HG Photos

Herman Linder putting on the ribbon during steer decorating at the Calgary Stampede.

Linder Collection

145

The Kainai Chieftainship

"...Got everything ready this a.m. to leave for the reserve to put in fence. Arrived around 8:30 p.m. Left for Owl Dance at John Cotton's and had big time. They gave me Indian name Calf Shirt."

—Linder diary, April 13, 1942

The old Chevrolet pick-up truck came to a stop as the headlight beams stabbed through the darkness of the cool Spring evening.

The lights picked up the figure of Emil Wings, a lithe Blood Indian, crouched close to the ground and studying the grass in the fork of the road. "We go this way," he said, pointing to the road on the right.

Rancher Herman Linder wondered at the accuracy of Emil's directions, nonetheless, shifting into gear and taking the trail towards a two-room house on the prairie where Indian men and women were congregating. Accompanying the young rancher were Emil Wings, wife Meggie and their son and daughter.

Winston Day Chief, a councillor with the Blood Tribe and Herman.

HG Photo

Ceremonial paint is applied to Herman's face by Wilton Goodstriker.

HG Photo

Herman was always being surprised by the people of the Blood tribe, who occupy the largest Indian reserve in Canada. Just a day earlier, he and Natives Chris Shade and Tom Prairie Chicken had been fencing on land leased from the Bloods when their vehicle quit on them. The men were four miles from camp with lots of work to be done. Herman was thinking of lost time and lost effort and the three hundred head of cattle that would soon be coming from his ranch at Cardston after a four-day trail drive.

His agitation was soothed by Chris, who reached into a coat pocket, palmed a small piece of glass and managed an Indian distress signal which was interpreted by tribe members some distance away. They soon came by horse to offer assistance.

But now it was time for the social evening to begin, one that would last well into the next morning. Indian ladies of all ages, sat on one side of the room, Herman and the other men stood opposite. Nervous, and not knowing what to expect, he was pleasantly surprised when two young women approached him, each taking an arm, as the drummers warmed to their task.

In his *Tribal Honours, A History of the Kainai Chieftainship* (1993), Hugh A. Dempsey

Herman visits with Chief Shot Both Sides and wife Rosalie during Kainai ceremonies.   *HG Photo*

said when the drumbeats start, two women — usually wives of councillors — go to the new members and they lead the dance around the circle. The Owl Dance is purely social and the invitations always come from the women. It is in bad form to refuse. A couple moves side by side, the man on the outside, his right arm over the woman's shoulder and his left hand holding her right hand in front of them. They do a slow "heel and toe" bobbing step as they move clockwise around the circle.

The drums no sooner stopped than Herman was approached by another Indian lady. Larger and older, she took the thirty-five-year-old rancher under her wing. From then on, he never missed an Owl Dance with many different partners.

When it was time to eat, Herman was treated as a special guest and served a plate of food. The other men rustled for themselves.

But something was afoot. Herman could sense that he was the object of much talk coming from a circle of Indian men. Suddenly, he was approached by Emil Wings and guided to the centre of the room. Attention was paid to George Strangling Wolf, a veteran of the First World War and respected warrior because of his overseas service. He spoke with a voice of authority saying that rancher Herman had always been a friend to the Bloods, was fair in his dealings with the tribe while leasing four sections of their land for summer range for his cattle and, finally, Herman Linder was a man known around the world as Mr. Cowboy.

The speech at an end, Herman was unceremoniously shoved away from the centre of the room, almost stumbling, so suddenly had the ceremony been terminated.

A great honour was accorded him that night as he was made an honourary member of the Blood Tribe of southern Alberta with the name of Oni-Stasi-Sokosimi, meaning Calf Shirt. Names come from former chiefs of the tribe. There were two chiefs by this name, probably uncle and nephew, wrote Dempsey.

"The first Calf Shirt had such a violent temper that he was given the nickname of Wild One. In 1859 he caused a feud by killing some of his own tribe. In 1865 he was one of the chiefs who wiped out the budding town of Ophir, Montana and in 1869 he tried to murder a Catholic priest. At the same time, he was recognized as one of the best warriors in the tribe. He was chief of the Lone Fighters band and died in the winter of 1873-1874 when gunned down by a whiskey trader.

"The second Calf Shirt was remembered because of his unique ability to handle rattlesnakes. The

Wilton Goodstriker, a member of the Horn Society speaks of Indian ways and Indian lore at a reception at the McIntyre Ranch.   *HG Photo*

Bloods detested and feared these reptiles, but Calf Shirt had a vision which gave him the power to handle them without being bitten. He became chief of the Crooked Backs band and made a living by putting on demonstrations with his snakes. He died in 1901."

The 1942 induction of Herman was repeated in a ceremony at the Lethbridge Flying Club in September, 1950, when Herman received a scroll signed by all the chiefs of the Blood tribe. It was then he was raised from Honourary Tribal Member to Honourary Chief. Forty-five years later, in the summer of 1995, Herman went through formal ceremonies at Standoff, Alberta which included face painting and receipt of an Indian headdress.

Horace Gladstone, left, and Emil Wings, Jr. reflect on Herman Linder. In the centre is a portrait of James Gladstone, Canada's first native senator.

HG Photo

The person deemed to be the first member of the Kainai Chieftainship was Edward, Prince of Wales (later Edward VIII) when, in 1919, he was given an Honourary Chieftainship. Head Chief Shot on Both Sides gave Edward the name Red Crow and placed upon his head a headdress which was to be worn on all official occasions. This was the start of a new chapter in the long standing tradition of granting to non-tribe individuals the

Bronze statue at the Blood administration centre at Standoff, Alberta honours Red Crow, the great chief who was a signatory to Treaty Number Seven. *HG Photo*

honour of serving the Blood Tribe as Honourary Chiefs.

During the ceremony the candidate is captured by a designated warrior and is seated on a buffalo robe, painted with ceremonial paint by a medicine man, and then give a headdress. The ceremony ends with the announcement of the adopted chief's name.

In the words of Dempsey: "The inductee comes to the Blood Reserve as an outsider, is captured, made a member and chief of the tribe, and leaves as a friend."

Dan Weasel Moccasin, a respected elder and councillor once said that when an individual went through the ceremony, had been awarded with an Indian name and headdress then no one could take the honour from him. The ceremony, he added, is religious by nature, full of meaningful symbolism, and the recipient and the ceremony were the objects of the Medicine Man's prayers.

The honour of becoming a chieftain was described in 1936 by Lord Tweedsmuir, the Governor General of Canada at that time, after he had been granted Chieftainship: "Today is the consummation of my youthful dreams. All my life I have been a fighting soldier. By admitting me in to your tribe you have given me the privilege of joining a band of warriors famous throughout the world for their bravery and prowess in arms."

The number of living people upon whom were bestowed this special honour grew until, in 1950, it was decided to form a society (Kainai Chieftainship) which could assist and advise the tribe. E.R. McFarland (Heavy Shield) became the first president. There can be no more than forty living members of the Kainai Chieftainship at any one time.

The object of the society is to assist the Blood Tribe in the preservation of their heritage as well as to promote educational, cultural, and economic development. Many of those honoured have served the tribe directly in one way or another.

Tribal drummers at a summer ceremony.

HG Photo

Nothing has changed with the Bloods in their respect for Herman after half-a-century.

"I have never heard anything negative about Mr. Linder. He is an honourable man," said Horace Gladstone, a son of Canada's first Indian senator, Jim Gladstone, also of the Blood tribe.

Emil Wings Jr. also had some good memories when Herman employed his dad and mom on the ranch, they tented there one summer and Herman taught the younger Wings to drive a truck.

"He was a good guy. He always treated us nice and was fair."

Herman ran about three hundred head of cattle on

Senator Joyce Fairbairn and Herman are two Honourary Kainai Chiefs. HG Photo

Indian lease land for five years, 1942-1946, and afterwards bought sufficient land at home to accommodate all his range needs.

He came away from the Indian reserve with a fine and warm impression of the tribal people.

It was in 1942 and he had engaged the services of eight Indians to help him put in posts and string wire, about eight miles west of where the University of Lethbridge now stands. He was sleeping in the tent with an Indian couple and their children the night of May 2 when a strong rain and wind storm swept in.

At some time in the night, Herman awoke with a start. The Indian husband was up and about in the tent. Herman lay still as the Indian came and stood over him. The next thing he knew the Indian was tucking the blankets around Herman's shoulder to protect him from the cold night air.

Said Herman: "That was something I have never forgotten. It was an act of kindness from one man to another. It was little, but it was much."

Tribute Dinner And Roast Held For Canada's Mister Rodeo

"...Got our rooms at the Lethbridge Lodge and the banquet started at 8 p.m. Everything was too wonderful for words. Went to Streeters party afterwards."

-Linder diary January 29, 1983

Cleve Hill, former Lethbridge (Alberta) Exhibition board member, held the spotlight when he spoke at a special roast for Herman during a Salute To Rodeo week in Lethbridge.

"Once I heard Herman talking to a group of cowboys about Maude, saying she had good eyes, carried her head high and had a full chest, well-formed rib-cage and nice legs. I thought, you Lutheran son-of-a-gun! Turned out he was talking about a mare at his ranch!"

Herman is seen to the right of Her Majesty Queen Elizabeth II and Prince Philip at the Royal Rodeo sponsored by the Calgary Exhibition and Stampede in October, 1951. Linder Collection

Hill also told the audience of four hundred that the Queen and Prince Philip visited Calgary on a rather cool day, October 18, 1951 and the Calgary Exhibition and Stampede staged a special rodeo for the Royal Couple.

"Herman was in the grandstand party and sat next to Her Majesty on a raw, cold day. He tucked a Hudson Bay blanket behind her to keep her warm, and gave her a little pat.

"Herman Linder is the only man, other than the Prince, in Canada, the British Commonwealth or the world, who has patted the Queen's derriere — that's how important he is," said Hill to roars of laughter.

The fun didn't end there ...

Ed O'Connor, past president of the Calgary Stampede, held a minute's silence immediately after he told the audience he was going to list Linder's good points.

Dalt Elton, master of ceremonies talked about Herman being "the old story of the little acorn growing into a big tree — which proves you never know how far a nut is going to go."

Herman's son-in-law and former Canadian rodeo great, Tom Bews, recalled the first time he saw Herman he was on a yellow horse, with a silver saddle and wearing a white stetson, looking just like movie star Rex Allen.

"Next time I saw him, I noticed this cute gal, his daughter Rosemarie...," said Bews, commonly known in his rodeo days as the Mayor of Pekisko and five-time Canadian All-Around cowboy.

Goldenrod author, Herb Harker, asked: "How can you honour a man who's not too smart? I figure I'm too smart to climb on a horse that I know is going to buck."

Rodeo stock contractor and Hall of Famer Reg Kesler suggested much of the success of rodeo is due to Herman Linder. "Without him we'd have

Chief Shot Both Sides and wife Rosalie of the Blood Tribe at tribute for Herman, the cowboy. *Alberta Beef Photo*

missed quite a part of rodeo in Canada and the United States."

Lethbridge exhibition board member and auctioneer Tony Perlich said "if ever there was a man that deserved to be honoured, Herman's it. He is a real hero."

Also present to honour Herman were: Ken Buxton of Claresholm, Alberta; and a longtime horseman, former world saddle bronc champion and Calgary arena director Winston Bruce; Indian rodeo greats Fred Gladstone and Rufus Goodstriker; Chinook Rodeo Association president Bob Wilson; steer wrestlers Tommy Ivins and Lee Phillips, president of the Canadian Professional Rodeo Association; and past rodeo star Harold Mandeville. It did Herman's heart good to see longtime friend and Calgary Stampede announcer Warren Cooper of Nanton, Alberta also there as well as famous trick roper Montie Montana.

Cowboy clown and movie star Slim Pickens couldn't make it because of illness, but actress and daughter, DaryleAnn Pickens, did. There was also a special presentation by Jim Shot Both Sides, former Chief of the Blood band, to Herman and wife Agnes.

Chairman for the roast was J.N. (Bus) Murdoch of Santa Barbara, California, who was filming a documentary on Herman's life, *A Man And His Dream*, at the time.

In reality it was more toasts than roasts.

Herman was taken back by many of the compliments.

"What can I say? I'm completely overwhelmed. Usually people wait until you're dead and gone before something like this — I keep pinching myself to see if I'm alive. There's no words in the dictionary to explain the feelings in my heart at this time."

He was happier, still, that the entire Linder family, including children and their spouses and grandchildren could attend the special event.

In answer to the tributes, Herman said: "The only thing I can think of to say, is that I pray God forgives them for telling all those lies and at the same time, I ask God to forgive me for believing them."

Alberta Maine-Anjou breeders paid tribute to Herman and Agnes Linder. From left are: Mr. and Mrs. Gary Smith, Wimborne; Mr. and Mrs. Rick Hillmer, Magrath; Dr. Al McKenzie, Edmonton; Agnes and Herman; Phyllis McKenzie, Edmonton; Mrs. and Mr. Robert Smith, Wimborne; Kia and George Linder, Cardston; and Rosemarie (Linder) Bews, Longview. *Alberta Beef Photo*

A Well-Deserved Tribute

One of the more eloquent tributes paid to Herman Linder came his way at a Dinner Roast held in his honour in Lethbridge, Alberta, January 29, 1983 and given by Cleve Hill, longtime friend and member of the Lethbridge and District Exhibition Board.

Here are some excerpts:

"Herman Linder — there in the annals of rodeo stands a giant! He is a champion, not 'just another' champion, he isn't 'just another' anything — in nothing he ever did, was Herman Linder 'just another' ...

"You have to travel away from Herman's home range to fully appreciate the respect this man commands. I had that privilege in 1973 when Agnes and Herman, accompanied Walter Hyssop, Dick and Carmel Gray and my wife Edith and myself to the National Finals in Oklahoma City. Herman had made all the arrangements: plane and rodeo tickets, hotel reservations, etc.

"Arriving at the hotel it took thirty minutes to get from the front door to the desk of the hotel, through the mass of people greeting Herman; everyone from a guy named Blevins, maker of Blevin saddle buckles from Wheatland, Wyoming, to Larry Mahan, Jim Shoulders and Freckles Brown!

"Forgive me if I paraphrase a few words which that great cowboy artist Charles M. Russell wrote of himself, quite a few years ago. They could truly be echoed in the life of tonight's honoured guest.

"The media have been kind to me — many more times more kind than true. Although I rodeo-ed for many years I am not what a lot of folks think a cowboy should be.

"My friends are mixed, cowboys, saints and sinners. I have always been what is called a good mixer. I had friends when I had nothing else. My friends were not always with the law, but I haven't said how law-abiding I was myself. I haven't been too bad — or too good — to get along with.

"Life has never been too serious with me. I lived to play and to a degree, I'm playing yet. Laughs and good judgment have saved me many a scrap, but I don't laugh at other's tears.

"I have always liked horses and have, for as long as I can remember, always owned a few. I believe in luck and have had lots of it.

"To have talent or ability is no credit to its owner. What a man can't help he should get neither credit nor blame for. It is not his fault.

"I am a cowboy and a rancher. There are lots better, some worse. Any man that can make a living doing what he likes is lucky and I'm that. Any time now that I cash in my chips, I win."

So Herman, Edith and I salute you, my dear friend, a real, downright, honest-to-God human being and again, in the words of the immortal Russell:

"May your days to come, be the best you've had
"Your wrinkles from laughs, not frowns.
"May your nights bring dreams that make you glad,
"And your joys be mountains, not mounds!"

Painting of Linder Goes To Cowboys

Ken Hurlburt of Fort Macleod, Alberta auctions oil painting of Herman on Easy Money. That's Warren "Coop" Cooper of Nanton assisting Hurlburt.

Alberta Beef Photo

An oil painting by Larry Christensen, showing Herman Linder aboard the big sorrel saddle bronc Easy Money, at the Calgary Stampede, sold for $3,000 at the Linder Roast January 28, 1983.

The painting, with Chief Mountain in the background, sold at a special auction at the end of a Linder tribute banquet at the Lethbridge Lodge Hotel.

Lee Phillips, president of the Canadian Professional Rodeo Association (CPRA), purchased the painting on behalf of the cowboy fraternity. It was taken to Calgary and placed in the CPRA headquarters where it hangs to this day.

He also spent $1,700 for a larger, back-lit print of the same picture.

"We bought the picture because we really feel Herman has done more for our cowboys than any other person we know of," Phillips said of the man who helped organize the Cowboys' Turtle Association, the first formal organization of rodeo contestants. It was a forerunner of the CPRA and the Professional Rodeo Cowboys Association of North America.

Phillips said Linder was a great champion and has worked his whole life to improve rodeo and the lot of the cowboy.

"We'd be totally wrong not to honour Herman any way we can," he said.

A second back-lit print was purchased at the roast by Fort Macleod Auction for $1,100. Auctioneer Ken Hurlburt promptly donated the art to the town of Cardston, to be hung in the Community Centre.

Thoughts Expressed On

Herman's Eightieth Birthday ... August 5, 1987

Cardston Mayor Larry Fiske congratulates Herman on his eightieth birthday. Looking on are auctioneer Ken Hurlburt and Tom and Rosemarie Bews.

Alberta Beef Photo

Ken Hurlburt
Fort Macleod-Highwood Auction Markets, Fort Macleod, Alberta

"Herman Linder is not only a great rodeo performer, but a great agriculturist. He's one of the greatest Canadians I have ever met. I was just getting started in the cattle business in 1947 and I made a deal with Herman and his brother Warner to buy a straight carload of cattle from me. One thing is for sure, if you ever made a deal with Herman, a deal's a deal. He's a tough old cookie, but a real gentleman."

Reg Kesler
Rosemary, Alberta, Rodeo Stock Contractor

"I was born at Lethbridge, October 15, 1919 and was eight or nine years old when I remember Herman riding a bucking horse at the Raymond (Alberta) Stampede. He helped put on the first rodeo at which I was a contestant. Herman is the father of modern rodeo in Canada. Without him, rodeo would have been in tough shape. He's one of the most colourful cowboys and arena directors I have ever known."

The Late Fritz Hanson
Calgary, Alberta

Hanson was a member of the 1948 Calgary Stampeder football team which claimed the Grey Cup that year, and member of the Canadian Football League Hall of Fame and Canadian Sports Hall of Fame and football player (halfback) for 23 years.

"I've known Herman since 1947. He was always a great Stampeder football fan and supported us very well. He's not only a great cowboy, but a most remarkable man."

Herman and Fritzie Hanson, former Calgary Stampeder great. Alberta Beef Photo

Rosemarie (Linder) Bews
Longview, Alberta, wife of former Canadian rodeo champion Tommy Bews.

"My dad's a tough old bird and we go back a long ways. He's kind, he's humble, he makes you feel better when you're in his company. He's a man of his word, fair and honest and always has something good to say about someone or something."

Gary Smith
Poplar Haven Ranch, Wimborne, Alberta

Past president, Canadian Maine-Anjou Association and former member, Alberta Canada All Breeds (cattle) Association (ACABA).

"I first met Herman in 1969 and he's been an inspiration to me and others. He has energy and ability and a good eye for cattle. We partnered up in Maine-Anjou cattle (LinderHaven) and it's been good for both us.

His energy is contagious and he exudes warmth and friendship. One could never begin to count Herman's friends, he just attracts people to him. When we visited Mexico on cattle business, he had the kind of reputation that was almost front-page news. He's an incredible man, reaching over many borders."

Warren Cooper

The Late Warren (Coop) Cooper
Nanton, Alberta, Infield voice of the Calgary Stampede for forty-two years.

"Herman has a great way with people. You realized that when we were at Expo '67 (World's Fair) in Montreal when Herman was rodeo manager and I was the announcer. Poor weather but the rodeo made money and we all had a lot of fun. A great cowboy, a great friend."

Joe Fisher
Medicine Hat, Alberta

Professional hockey player with the Detroit Red Wings for five years and longtime cowman and past president, Medicine Hat Exhibition and Stampede.

"My wife Gertie and myself have been fortunate to have been guests of the Linder family. They are charming hosts, gracious and courteous. There are not enough words

Joe Fisher, left, of Medicine Hat and Jack McCulloch of Calgary at Herman's eightieth birthday party.   *Alberta Beef Photo*

to describe Herman Linder, but he will forever be an honoured guest of the Medicine Hat Stampede."

The Late Dick Gray
Lethbridge, Alberta

Founding president, Alberta Cattle Feeders' Association, owner Valley Feeders, Lethbridge for twenty-two years and past president of the Lethbridge Exhibition and Stampede.

"I go back to pre-World War Two days when men like Harry Minor and Gene Burton were selling grass steers for two and one-half cents a pound. Herman has good cattle sense and knows how prices can change from one year to the next. He's not only an All-Around cowboy and arena director, but a man who knows the value of a dollar. I was president of the Lethbridge Exhibition board when Herman was named to our Sports Hall of Fame ... an honour well earned."

Herman, Ernie Nimitz, George Linder and the late Dick Gray of Lethbridge.

Herman visits Premier Joey Smallwood, right, in Newfoundland. Herman holds Smallwood's grandchild, Dale Russell. At left is Smallwood's son-in-law Edward.
Linder Collection

In his book, The Time Has Come To Tell, *the late Joseph R. Smallwood, former Premier of Newfoundland, had this to say about Herman Linder:*

I Knew The World's
Greatest Cowboy

"Herman Linder was champion cowboy of Canada, of the United States, of Australia, of the world.

"My son-in-law Edward Russell and I went to see him on his ranch the other side of Cardston in Alberta. On our way there we passed by the great and reputedly breathlessly beautiful Mormon temple, and on the ranch we bought two saddle horses from Linder — I, a Palomino, and my son-in-law, a quarter horse. They travelled by train all the way to my home at Roache's Line a few weeks later.

"I had my movie camera with me, and Herman Linder put on a special, spectacular show for me on his ranch: he leaped into the saddle of his horse and galloped toward a racing calf, lassoed the animal, sprang to the ground, roped its four legs — all in championship time. I have the movie somewhere still.

"Herman Linder accepted my invitation to visit Newfoundland, and I had the fun of showing him about on some of our barrens on the Avalon Peninsula."

(Newfoundland Book Publishers 1967 Ltd.
St. John's, Newfoundland.)

An Iowa Accolade

When the big rodeo show at Sidney, Iowa, celebrated its Fiftieth Anniversary in 1973, the American Legion Post, which sponsored it, put out a book describing how the show got started and naming the big-time rodeo stars who had competed there over the years.

In the history of their event, said the book, two cowboys had dominated the competitions: before the Second World War it was Herman Linder of Cardston, Alberta and afterwards it was Jim Shoulders of Henrietta, Oklahoma.

Sunshine And Shadow At Year's End

Herman Linder has kept a daily diary of events since 1932 and much of his rodeo and ranching history are found in these log books.

Sad times and happy times are reflected in these pages, the story of four generations and the country that helped to shape them.

Dec. 31, 1935   "A good and bad year. Won Brahma bull riding at Calgary and North American and Canadian All-Around championships. But also got hurt bad at Boston Garden rodeo when Big Boy bucked me off. In hospital several days."

Dec. 31, 1936   " A special rodeo year for the Linder brothers at the Calgary Stampede. Brother Warner won the calf roping and the steer decorating and I won bareback and Brahma bull riding titles as well as North American and Canadian All-Around championships. Also had several wonderful weeks at a rodeo in Australia with Agnes."

Dec. 31, 1939   " Just concluded one of the greatest years of our lives. We had the pleasure of moving into our new home, electric lights and all. We are very happy. Very successful and prosperous year all-around. Made decision to give up riding roughstock at rodeos and got a great thrill in judging rodeo at Madison Square Garden."

Dec. 31, 1942   "The month of June was one of the coldest and rainiest in history. September was also bad as we had ninety aces of wheat snowed down and froze the heck out of most of our grain."

Dec. 31, 1943   "Was a prosperous year but the saddest of our lives. Had many troubles all year. We miss our daddy so awfully much."

Dec. 31, 1944   "Our most prosperous year to date. A real banner year with a beautiful daughter added to our family June 18."

Dec. 31, 1955   "Threshing was going well until our straw stack caught fire and we just got the machinery away in time. Many neighbours came to help."

Dec. 31, 1959   "First year since we have been to Canada that we had grain that wasn't harvested. Was a pretty good year, all in all."

Dec. 31, 1960   "Some good things in rodeo and some heartaches. The first year in our life we were through harvesting in August. A dry year as a whole."

Dec. 31, 1961   "Started out very dry, but later got enough rain to make this a good year. Cattle prices stayed up. Winnipeg rodeo was very disappointing."

Dec. 31, 1962   "Our hardest year, but later turned out the best. Our son George came through two heart operations. The second quarter was a trying one. Almost losing George, hired man left and then the old house burned down. But it ended in a blaze of abundance of good health and many worldly blessings."

Dec. 31, 1963   "A most unusual year. Nice winter, then a severe drought, then lots of rain and then drought again. Exceptionally nice fall with no frost until very late. One of the best crops since we have been in Canada (1918). Fat cattle prices disappointing.

Dec. 31, 1965   "A very hard year for both my honey and I. Around one hundred days on my back. The big event was Rosemarie's wedding to Tommy Bews. Real good crops and done exceptionally well with our steers.

Dec. 31, 1966   "A wonderful year for crops, grass and hay. Steers turned out really good, very good prices. Our labour gave us a bad time. The real big event was getting the contract for the rodeo at Expo '67 in Montreal.

Dec. 31, 1967   "Worst spring ever, grass and hay was good but crops were poor. Spent almost a month in the Fort Macleod hospital after rodeo accident. Expo was a great experience. Lost nine big steers, feeder burned down. Was a bad and also a good year."

Dec. 31, 1968 "A very cool summer with lots of rain. A very late harvest but a very good one. We had many records broken: cold, moisture, the heaviest snowfall in history in September."

Dec. 31, 1972 "The winter of 1971-72 was one of the hardest winters we have ever had since we have been in Canada. Lots of snow. However 1972 was a good year for crops, hay and grass. Prices were very good, so all in all it was a very good year. We seemed to have a heavy loss in our cattle. First big blow was when we lost our purebred bull."

Dec. 31, 1973 "This will go down as one of the drier years we have had since we came here in 1918. In fact it was a year very much like 1918. Many things to be thankful for. We have everything that we need for our physical well being. Were able to buy enough hay for our stock, even though it was very high. Everything is going well."

Dec. 31, 1980 "Good rains and trip to Mexico with Alberta Canada All Breeds Association. Wonderful crop and prices of grain good. Cattle prices fair. The two real highlights of the year to be inducted into the Alberta Sports Hall of Fame and to top it off to be inducted into the Cowboy Hall of Fame in Oklahoma City."

Dec. 31, 1982 "Another special year. Being asked to open the Calgary Exhibition and Stampede was a big honour. Also inducted into the Canadian Cowboy Hall of Fame. There was a documentary film done on the Linder Ranch. Hay crop was short and grain crops fair. Our health was good which is the greatest blessing of all. Our great fiftieth wedding anniversary was wonderful with so many of our friends coming to celebrate."

Dec. 31, 1983 "This was a bad year. Hailed out and dried out. Terribly hot. A bull knocked my horse down in the pasture and broke my hip and wrecked my knee. While I was in Lethbridge hospital, Warner, Rozella and Agnes came to visit me and as they were leaving a car hit them and broke some of Agnes' ribs while Rozella had eleven stitches put in her face and Warner was badly shaken up. Got word

sister-in-law Christine died and we went to South Dakota for her funeral. After all this, we lost brother Warner October 27. Was a great loss to me."

Dec. 31, 1985 "I ran across something my dear wife wrote before she went to be with the Lord April 27. It was called *No Sad Tears For Me, Please*. So sad. It really broke me up and I just couldn't help but shed tears. Granddaughter Nancy came over for a while this eve and we shed tears together. I miss Mother so much. So all alone in this house ..."

Dec. 31, 1986 "Will remember January 5. Was sitting in Mother's rocker on Sunday morning when granddaughter Nancy came running in and told me to come quick as her dad (George) was feeding cattle and is now under the truck. I rushed out and Nancy was driving the truck to the field where daughter-in-law Kia was with George. It was a terrible shock. George really looked like he was gone. Kia tried so hard to revive him. The ambulance came and took him to town. They phoned that my son George had gone over the Great Divide. A very sorrowful day."

On February 21, 1987, Herman attended a special roast for longtime friend and Champion Calf Roper Fred Gladstone. From left: Jim Gladstone, Hugh Dempsey, Herman Linder, Edith and Fred Gladstone, Howard Bly, unidentified, Stan Walker, Howard Potter, Harold Mandeville. *Alberta Beef Photo*

Linder The Prose Man

Favored Selections From The Book Of Linder

"... Did all the chores and went to town to go with Reeder to look at some more hay. Bought ten ton. Brought coal home. Agnes and I went to Tom Duce's for a party. Snowed some."

- Linder diary, January 19, 1945

Among the qualities possessed by Herman are his love of people, modesty and appreciation for all things great and small. He'll take a "cup" at places like the Rangeman's Dinner at the Palliser Hotel in Calgary during Stampede week, reminisce with the dying breed of cowboys from his younger days, and go from here to Hell and back to attend a rodeo.

Often, with friends, he'll slip into a poetic mood and recite poems that will move an audience. His memory is uncanny, his gift of oratory most compelling.

Here are some of his favorites:

Herman makes another entry in his diary — something he has done each night for sixty-five years. HG Photo

A Toast To Life

Here's to life with its crooked street, here's to death we all must meet
Now if life were a thing, that wealth could buy,
The rich would live and the poor would die.
But God in His wisdom made it so, that rich or poor, we all must go
So here's to life. Let's enjoy!   Anon

The Burglar Bold

The story I tell of a burglar bold
Who started to rob a house
He opened the window and crept in
As quiet as any mouse.

He looked around the room
For a place to hide
Until the folks were all asleep
Then, said he, with their money
I'll take a quiet sneak.

So under the bed the burglar went
He crept up close to the wall
It happened to be an old maid's room
Or he wouldn't have had the gall.

At nine o'clock the old maid came in
"I'm so awfully tired," she said
She thought that all was well that night
And never looked under the bed.

She took out her teeth and big glass eye
And the hair all off of her head
The burglar he had forty fits
As he watched from under the bed.
From under the bed the burglar crept

He was a total wreck
But the old maid wasn't asleep at all
She grabbed him by the neck.

She didn't shout or holler or call
She was as cool as a clam
She only said: "The Saints be praised"
At last I've found a man.

From under the pillow, a gun she drew
And to the burglar she said
"Young man, if you don't marry me
"I'll blow off the top of your head.

The burglar looked around the room
There wasn't a place to scoot
He looked at her teeth and her big glass eye
And the hair all off her head, and said:
"Madam, for gosh sakes shoot!

—Anon

Getting Forgetful

Just a line to say I'm living,
That I'm not among the dead
Though I'm getting more forgetful
And mixed up in my head.

For sometimes I can't remember,
As I stand at the foot of the stairs
If I must go up for some thing
Or if I just came down from there.

I'm before the refrigerator so often,
My poor mind is filled with doubt,
Have I just put the food away
Or come to take it out?

I've got used to my arthritis,
To my dentures I'm resigned;
I can manage my bifocals
But, Oh God, I miss my mind...

And there are times when it is dark out,
With my night cap on my head,
I don't know if I'm retiring
Or just getting out of bed.

So if it's my turn to write you,
There is no need for getting sore
I may think that I have written
And don't want to be a bore.

So remember that I love you
And wish that you were here,
But now it's nearly mailtime
And I must say Good-bye my Dear.

Now I stand beside the mailbox
With a face so very red,
Instead of mailing you my letter
I've opened it instead.

—Anon

Code Of The Cow Country

It don't take such a lot of laws
To keep the rangeland straight,
Nor books to write 'em in, because
There's only six or eight.
The first one is the welcome sign —
True brand of western hearts;
"My camp is yours and yours is mine,"
In all cow country parts.

Treat with respect all womankind,
Same as you would your sister,
Take care of neighbors' strays you find,
And don't call cowboys "Mister."
Shut pasture gates when passin' through,
And takin' all in all,
Be just as rough as pleases you,
But never mean nor small.

Talk straight, shoot straight and never break
Your word to man nor boss.
Plumb always kill a rattlesnake
Don't ride a sorebacked hoss.
It don't take law nor pedigree
To live the best you can!
These few is all it takes to be
A cowboy — and a man!

—Anon

Two People Together

Five years after he lost his first wife Agnes, to a brain tumor, Herman took the hand of Chicago-born Adeline Tellesch in marriage in the Lutheran Church at Cut Bank, Montana.

The marriage was performed May 26, 1990. The groom was eighty-three and the bride, seventy-eight. Each had lost a spouse prior to their second marriage and they had been acquainted for several years. Adeline is the mother of one son, Wayne, and Herman the father of two: George (deceased) and Rosemarie (Mrs. Tom Bews).

The couple took up residence at the Linder Ranch, six miles west of Cardston and Adeline developed a deep interest in rodeo and quickly became a fan of arena events.

Since their marriage, the couple has travelled widely to many points in Canada and the United States, attending rodeos and meetings of the Rodeo Historical Society of America. Their last travels took them to the Hawaiian Islands in February, 1996. Herman stopped there in 1936 and again in 1938 on his way to rodeo competitions in Australia sponsored by the Royal Agricultural Society of Sydney.

The Linders have also maintained an interest in Maine-Anjou cattle and Herman still runs Maines under the name LinderHaven (with the Smith brothers) of Wimborne, Alberta.

Adeline has an effervescent personality and has been one of Herman's greatest rodeo fans the past six years.

Herman and Adeline with Cardston's Faith Lutheran pastor James Lindemann.
HG Photo

Herman and Adeline ... on the rodeo trail.
DS Photo

"The two best things that can happen to a man is to have a good wife and be accepted by the people he comes from." ... American Cowboy Poet and Humourist Will Rogers

September, 1950 Calf Shirt (Oni-Stasi-Sokosimi), Honourary Chief of the Blood Tribe of the Blackfoot Confederacy, Kainai Chieftanship.

August 21, 1957 Inductee, National Cowboy Hall of Fame and Western Heritage Center, Oklahoma City, Oklahoma.

December, 1957 Named Outstanding Committee Man For The Year by International Rodeo Association.

1960 Honourary Life President, Canadian Stampede Managers' Association.

November 15, 1961 Made an Honourary Citizen of the town of Fort Macleod, Alberta. He was presented with a beautiful desk and chair (still in use in his office) by its citizens for his involvement and support of rodeo in the community.

June, 1962 Life Member, Canadian Cowboys' Protective Association.

October 18, 1967 Honourary Citizen, Winnipeg, Manitoba.

1968 Life Member, Benevolent and Protective Order of Elks, Lodge 34.

1970 Special Service Award, Calgary Exhibition and Stampede.

September, 1971 Master Farm Family Award, Province of Alberta, Department of Agriculture, 1971. *"Herman Linder Family — Good Farming, Right Living, Clear Thinking."*

October 28, 1971 Southern Alberta Rodeo Circuit Appreciation Trophy for services to the field of rodeo, 1948-1970.

December 7, 1972 "The National Cowboy Hall of Fame and Western Heritage Center - Resolution - *Be it hereby known that the Board of Directors of the Rodeo Historical Society after due consideration, has selected Herman Linder of Cardston, Alberta*

Herman Linder, eighty-nine years of age, August 5, 1996
Dorothea Schaab Photo

Canada as the 1972 Man of the Year of said Society, and does heartily commend him for his exceptional efforts in behalf of the Society and presents to him this day a bronze medallion in token of its appreciation. Dated this seventh day of December, 1972, Oklahoma City, Oklahoma."

1973 Herman asked to dinner by the board of the Red Deer Exhibition Association. It was then he was presented with a silver spur mounted on a plaque which read: *"To Mr. Rodeo, Herman Linder, for his outstanding contributions to the world of rodeo as well as being an unexcelled Goodwill Ambassador Red Deer Exhibition Association 1973."*

November 7, 1975 Alberta Maine-Anjou (beef cattle) Association Man of the Year.

1975 On two different occasions, the Professional Rodeo Cowboys Association of the United States has made presentations to Herman Linder for his continued support of rodeo. The first one, presented in 1975 reads: *"Rodeo Cowboys Association, Inc. presented to Herman Linder for continued support to professional rodeo, From the Board of Directors, PRCA 1975."*

1975 A second plaque, without date, reads: *"A turtle never got anywhere if he didn't stick his neck out."* Presented by the Professional Rodeo Cowboys Association to Herman Linder in recognition of his efforts towards raising the standards of the sport of rodeo."

July 22, 1976 The Lethbridge Exhibition Board chooses Linder to officially open their rodeo July 22, 1976 commemorating the eightieth anniversary (1896-1976) of the Fair in the southern Alberta city. Herman was also named to the Lethbridge Hall of Fame.

April 11, 1979 Honourary Member, Fort Macleod Rotary Club.

October 11, 1980 Inductee, Alberta Sports Hall of Fame.

November 10, 1982 Second Contestant Inductee, Canadian Rodeo Hall of Fame.

1982 Honourary Member, Royal Canadian Legion Branch, Cardston.

1985 Honourary Member, Cardston Rotary Club.

1986 Life Member, Calgary Exhibition and Stampede.

November 7, 1987 A framed certificate is presented to Herman when named Cardston and District's Male Athlete of the Century. It reads in part: *"Cardston's Centennial Hall of Fame, November 7, 1987 Presented to Herman Linder Rodeo Champion Cowboy 1929-1939; Rodeo Judge 1940-1943; Arena Director 1944-1969; Alberta Sports Hall of Fame 1980; Most Outstanding Male Athlete Of The Century. Signed: Willard Brooks, Chairman, Hall of Fame Committee."*

December 10, 1987 Among the honours accorded Herman was a surprise presentation of a calf-hide scroll at the National Rodeo Finals in Las Vegas, Nevada in 1987. It reads: *"Honouree of the Year Presented to Herman Linder Cowboys' Turtle Association No. 22. A tribute of appreciation in honour and recognition of your dedication to rodeo. The ability and experience you have shown throughout the years in your chosen profession is expressed here today by all those who love and respect you. ProRodeo Historical Society December 10, 1987 Las Vegas, Nevada."*

January, 1993 Herman awarded the Commemorative Medal for the 125th anniversary of Canadian Confederation. The award is given to people who have made a significant contribution to Canada, to their community or to their fellow Canadians. The decoration is a reminder of the values of service, individual respect, and community effort on which Canada was built and on which its quality of life will always depend.

Herman with some reminders of yesteryears.

Memories From Across The Years

If one wants to know the Herman Linder story, then visit his den, his office, or the family living room. Medals and mementos of the past speak of rodeo days of yore and a thousand friendships.

In the past, there were eleven belt buckles — many gold, seventeen presentation watches, pearl-handled jackknives and a watch fob from the Rodeo Association of America, which speak of early championships south of the border, a small lapel button with a turtle, and pictures and scrapbooks galore.

The little copper turtle button is special. Very special. It is the size of a ten-cent piece and probably cost about the same. But it had a profound meaning for rodeo contestants who were often at the mercy of shrewd promoters, and pedestrian judges who knew nothing about the sport of rodeo. The turtle was a rallying symbol at Boston Garden in 1936, forever changing the face of rodeo in North America. A band of cowboy strikers, sixty-one in number, would adopt the turtle as their emblem because they, too, were slow to organize and get going.

The Linder Ranch at Cardston, Alberta was sold to this young family May 19, 1993. Brad Beazer, seated, and wife Lydia are seen with sons Chad, 12, and Daylin, 10, and daughters Rachel, 9, and Jenae, 7. During 1996 a new house was built on the home quarter for the Beazers while Herman and wife Adeline still occupy the original ranchhouse.
HG photo.

There's history aplenty at the Linder ranch west of Cardston and although he's a modest man, Herman lives and breathes rodeo as much today as when he put spurs and chaps to a bucking bronc over three continents.

A good many of his trophies and saddle and chaps now rest in cowboy Halls of Fame in the United States and Canada such as Oklahoma City, Colorado Springs, Lewiston, Idaho; and in Alberta at Red Deer, Cochrane's Western Heritage Centre and Calgary's Glenbow Museum.

Rodeo photos from yesteryear speak of New York, where Herman competed and judged; Boston, where the strike took place; Chicago and Sidney, Iowa in the United States. Through Canada they include: Williams Lake, Penticton and Vancouver, British Columbia; Fort Macleod, Medicine Hat, Lethbridge, Edmonton, and many smaller communities in Alberta; Winnipeg and Swan River, Manitoba; and Montreal, Quebec; and a large number of other points on the North American map, as well as international events in Australia and England.

Stars from other sports also adorn the walls. Jockey George "Iceman" Woolf, hockey star Gordie Howe, and rodeo greats like Casey Tibbs, Johnnie Schneider, Pete Knight and Canada Kid are in great company with men like Calgary Stampede announcer Warren Cooper and rodeo clown Slim Pickens.

There's also three guest books, pages yellowed from the years, filled with names of friends and celebrities from throughout the world.

Although there are seven grandchildren and a number of great grandchildren, no one will carry on the Linder name. Son George's three children were all girls, daughter Rosemarie's four boys will carry the Bews name and although married, brother Warner never had any children.

The Linder Ranch was sold in May, 1993 to a young Cardston couple and Herman and Adeline remain on the ranch at the time of this writing.

In rodeo and ranch circles, the Linder name belongs to the ages.

165

The Author

Harald Gunderson

Harald Gunderson is a son of the Western prairies and knows the smell of sagebrush and the plaintive call of the coyote.

Born in Maple Creek, Saskatchewan, "The Little Cowtown of the West," he recalls there were ranchers, cowboys and Indians to the south and dryland farmers to the north. He remembers, as a youngster, watching the encampments of the Cree, their colourful teepees and the flickering flames of their evening fires.

Maple Creek was proud of its yearly Stampede and it was here that Gunderson first learned to appreciate the whirlwind action of the rodeo infield and watched as spirited men and horses gave their explosive performances. It was also in Maple Creek that the author would win his first start in rodeo as boy's steer riding champion in 1944.

Educated in Maple Creek and Medicine Hat, Alberta, he became a newspaper reporter and covered Stampede infield events for both *The Medicine Hat News* and *The Calgary Herald*. He later established a publishing company which included two cattle magazines: *The World of Beef* and *Limousin Leader*.

Gunderson remembers Herman Linder as a rodeo director, "while I was just a kid," and the two later became fast friends through Herman's involvement in commercial and purebred cattle and Gunderson as a cattle publisher. Their friendship has lasted twenty-five years, even though there's a "fierceness" in their cribbage matches.

"*The Linder Legend — The Story of ProRodeo and its Champion,*" has been two years in the making and allowed Gunderson to make numerous visits to the Linder Ranch, where most of the research for the book has been completed.

Gunderson and Shirley, his wife of forty-eight years, reside in Calgary. They have four children (a son, Lee, is with *Alberta Beef Magazine*), and nine grandchildren.